RUPERT
A Bear's Life

THIS BOOK
BELONGS TO

A Bear's Life

RUPERT

GEORGE PERRY with Alfred Bestall

PAVILION
MICHAEL JOSEPH

ACKNOWLEDGEMENTS

The illustrations in this book have been supplied from the following sources:

Express Newspapers PLC
Alan and Laurel Clark
Alfred Bestall
MPL Communications Ltd.

Special thanks are due to Lawrence Edwards for his design and picture editing, Jenny de Gex for the picture research, Alan and Laurel Clark for their helpful advice and the run of their magnificent collection of 'Rupertiana', James Henderson of the *Daily Express* for his constructive advice, Peter Knight of the *Daily Express* for inspiring the book initially, Colin Webb of Pavilion for having the foresight to publish it, my wife Frances, and particularly my son Matthew for his technical consultancy, but most of all to Alfred Bestall MBE for his indefatigable enthusiasm, kindness and treasure trove of memories and artifacts.

First published in Great Britain in 1985
By Pavilion Books Limited
196 Shaftesbury Avenue, London WC2H 8JL
in association with Michael Joseph Limited
44 Bedford Square, London WC1B 3DP

Designed by Lawrence Edwards

British Library Cataloguing in Publication Data
Perry, George, 1935–
  Rupert, a bear's life
  1. Bestall, Alfred   2. Rupert (Cartoon character)
  I. Title
  741.5′942   PN6738.R8

ISBN 0-907516-76-9

Printed in Italy by Grafica Editoriale

CONTENTS

*For Rupert's chums,
however old or young
they may be*

In And Out of the Shops.

THE pleasure of the frock the better is still the order of the day with most of the smartest day dresses. Silk braid is playing a very prominent part in the trimming of the daintier cloth dresses, and it is interesting to note the return of the braided hem at the bottom of the skirt, which is one of the newest notes.

Accordion-pleated crêpe de Chine is now being much used, as also is ninon, a note of the shops. Delightful petticoats are showing frocks to be made of a nice material, trimmed with shadow lace and ribbon flowers, and the total cost is surprisingly small, if they are made at home.

Beautiful fur coat models of the latest and most novel cut and very handsome skins are being shown now at Burberry's. Fashion decrees that every smart fur coat shall be tailor-made to every direction, but collar, big sleeve, and hanging in soft lines. The same line is also showing a quantity of delightful children's fur coats and fur-lined coats for men.

The children's work trade, an industry that has been typically British from its very inception, is the latest mark for foreign competition, so I hear in the shops.

The trouble is, so the head of the largest manufacturers of children's works in this country, the firm responsible for making over 8,000 pairs of Jason's socks and thereupon for three years past, explained, that none of the foreign marks which come to this country bear any identification mark.

What is more, it appears that it is open to any one here to brand these foreign goods in any way they like, and parents are being misled and disappointed in consequence, for there is an enormous amount of inferior goods included among these objectionable imports.

"Ask where the goods come from." This is the advice of the expert, and if women renders will do this, a great British industry will be saved from unfair competition.

I have seen the coolest brushed wool sets, comprising a comfortable little pull-on hat, a scarf with a large pom-pon at each end, and a pillow muff, quilted and a lit lined that set in a pretty shade of fawn grey looked exactly like expensive squirrel at a distance. Equally attractive are wrap, and had in dark grey and bigger brown at four guineas.

Soft deep pink hats of suede and velour cloth are being worn a great deal just now. They make an attractive foil to the darkness of fur coats and dark suits. Equally attractive hats of the brilliant order are those lovely turbans of brilliant blue and exquisite chiffon velvet. These are most effective when worn by the dark girl with the clear, pallid type of complexion.

The little lace frocks are still persisting in popularity. Grey and silver lace is very lovely, but so are all the ecru and biscuit shades; and the lace which has been dyed rose and Nattier blue makes fascinating frocks.

Really good shoes are always so economy, even when the price is high, for they are a protection to health as well as an aid to smartness. When boots and shoes of the highest grade are reduced from £3 13s. to four £7 5s., and from £2 15s. to a uniform 21s. a pair, then indeed are there bargains going. This is what is happening at three branch establishments of Messrs W. Abbott and Sons this week.

These bargains are single pair oddment boots and shoes from the firm's London and Paris shops, and they include in patent, glacé, calf, and suede leather. The three branches where the special sale will be in session are those at 121, High Holborn, 51, Regent-street, and 69, Strand.

Narrow black ribbon is being used to trim some of the newest satin lingerie, and it is really very effective. The prettiest garments are on very ornament of lace and frills that the black ribbon adds just a note of smartness.

Inexpensive lingerie that is at the same time dainty and well finished is to be found in great variety at Robinson and Cleaver's, who are making a specialty of these reasonably-priced garments. There are also some of those popular knitted frocks in lovely Nattier blue, Quaker grey, mauve, brown, and orange, which are to be had at ridiculously low prices.

An assortment of beautiful coats, some selling as low as five guineas, made of velour cloth and of excellent cut, are another interesting find at this same shop.

Far in becoming quite a steady companion to the jumper. Beautiful silk-knitted ones of rose and turquoise blue are being trimmed with a white fox fur or bands of skunk, self-knitted ones are also enhanced by fur trimming.   M. H. L.

Art of the Spanish Comb.

The opening of the Exhibition of Spanish Art at Burlington House is having a decided effect on women's fashions in general, and long earrings and high combs are making their appearance in increasing numbers. The idea of wearing a crimson rose at the ear is also finding favour with evening coiffures.

Raquel Meller, the Spanish dancer and singer, it may be recalled, always wore one of these combs when appearing on the stage—and of.

There has been a great rush to buy them, and women are finding much difficulty in procuring choice tortoiseshell specimens. They are rare, and consequently much sought after.

The Hon. Mrs. John Fortescue has a particularly fine collection of these precious old Spanish combs, and women who have admired the high Spanish comb, prettily because the back of their combs, find it impossible to lightly down to the old, and have found it chilly away at the temples, in having an ordinary "cold" comb of the face, in order to support the comb.

This comb must be worn upright or nearly, and it must be admitted that, placed in the latter position, the effect is much more natural and striking.

Heads, cut of most as the original combs are all Carmen, and like many hundreds of pretty Spanish girls' heads, the explanation being that the Baroness e ... the best round the type and subsequently into China. Their "head" need have comprised many of these combs.

It is a common fallacy that fair women would wear the high Spanish comb, principally because the hair of their combs is people with dark-haired maids, but if a blond comb is selected there is no reason why the tortoiseshell women should not indulge in the prevailing fashion.

WHAT SHOULD SHE BE?

XI.—A CHAUFFEUSE.

MANY ex-service V.A.D.'s have obtained posts as chauffeuses to doctors, who are thus able to call them if needing assistance with patients. Although it is not essential for a doctor's chauffeuse to be also a V.A.D., the combination is a useful one, and ought to be borne in mind by ex-V.A.D.'s who want a more or less outdoor life.

The numbers of women that may be seen driving motors in London traffic and everywhere else are sufficient proof of the aptitude for women chauffeurs. The highest remuneration is about £2 a week, with board and lodging, or £2 to £4 a week, but the outdoor life is very healthy.

Instruction in mechanics as and the knowledge of electrical knowledge for the necessary R.A.C. certificate can be obtained at a cost of £5 5s. to £15 5s. for a monthly tuition at any of the schools recommended by the Royal Automobile Club, including the following:—

The Motor Training Institute, Baldwin-terrace, Bayswater, W.; The Ladies' School of Motoring, W.; Mary Ellen's place, Kensington, W., the Warwick School of Motoring, Warwickroad, Hammersmith, W.

The Breakfast Problem.

Now that eggs are so expensive, the problem of how to avoid something in the breakfast menu worries many housewives.

Try this trio of breakfast dishes, all of which may be prepared beforehand and only require reheating in the morning.

SARDINES AND TOMATO RICE.

Ingredients: 1lb. of rice, 4 sardines, 1lb. of tomatoes, salt, pepper, 2oz. of margarine, 1 gill of milk.

Method: Put the rice into boiling salted water and boil until soft, but not sticky. Drain well. Keep the water for consommé stock

or to use in place of starch. Remove the skin and bones from the sardines, and break them up into a fluid. Put the tomatoes into boiling water for five minutes, then remove the skins and slice them. Melt the margarine in a pan, add the tomatoes, cook over gentle heat for eight minutes, add the rice, sardines, milk, and reasoning, and stir until hot. Pile on a hot dish and serve.

HERRING BALLS.

Ingredients: 4 of cooked herring, 4lb of mashed potatoes, 1 or 2 tablespoonfuls of milk, 1 teaspoonful of chopped parsley, salt, pepper, breadcrumbs.

Method: Remove the skin and bones from the herrings and mash it up with a fork. Boil the potatoes through a sieve or mash them, and mix with the fish, parsley, and seasoning. Add enough milk to bind them. Flour the hands and roll the mixture into balls, brush them over with milk, coat with breadcrumbs, and fry pale brown in hot fat. Drain on a dish, and garnish with fried parsley. The balls may be prepared the previous day and fried in the morning.

CURRY TOAST.

Ingredients: 4oz. of cooked meat or fish, 1oz. of margarine, 1oz. of flour, 1 teaspoonful of curry powder, 1 small onion, 1 apple, salt, 1 pint of stock.

Method: Cut the meat into dice, or remove the skin and bones from the fish and flake it. Peel and mince the onion, peel and core and mince the apple. Melt the margarine in a pan, add the onion and apple, and fry till soft. Stir in the flour, curry powder, and the stock gradually, and let it boil. Add the meat or fish, and season. Simmer for twenty minutes. Serve on squares of hot toast.

Careers—and How to Choose Them.

Many mothers and daughters who are following the What Should She Be? series of notes now appearing on this page have difficulty asking where they can obtain fuller information about some chosen career. The answer to all such inquiries will be found in this article.

If you should decide to go to the Central Bureau for the Employment of Educated Women for advice on the subject of a career, you must not enter the building with any idea of the calling you think you are best fitted for.

This sounds superfluous advice, but those in charge of the office at 3, Princes-street, Cavendish-square, will tell you that sometimes women drift in without any definite idea about suitable work in their heads and leave again with all particulars and advice about some career they had never thought of which offers just the opening of any sort. Others have easy to admit with any that they would like to do poultry-farming, and will suddenly change their chosen vocation or something utterly different, say, dentistry or dancing, before they leave the bureau.

People totally unsuited for certain careers, sometimes cling with tenacity to the idea of a profession in which they would be doomed to fail. A woman with a bad complexion and an indifferent figure could not be dissuaded from seeking training as a beauty specialist.

PRACTICAL HINTS.

"Where can I live?" is the most often heard question at the bureau. This is a difficult query to answer satisfactorily, but the girls are given addresses of good boarding houses, hostels, and clubs whenever possible, although the bureau is distinctly not a house agency.

Several simple points to women seeking employment are given by the secretary of the bureau thus:—

"(1) Be open-minded as to what you want to do and what you are best fitted before you call.

"(2) If money is necessary to start you and to equip you for your training, or least fund may be of assistance to you.

"(3) Don't try this thing: for which you are obviously unsuited. For instance, it is useless to think of starting a high-class enterprise with no previous knowledge of business experience and no capital to start on.

"It is useless to want to establish a knitting shop if you are ignorant from the centre and have no idea of fashion," explained the secretary. "You draw and sell in baby works without any knowledge or branch of handicrafts, expect the art training or floor and others millinery cannot to open a shop at once with no previous knowledge of training; of course, no-devoted the expect doing any such things."

"Home decoration, cookery tea shop, poultry-farming, library work, and secretarial school teaching, are some of the more interesting and most popular careers for which training is being asked about at the moment."

"There is women are finding good openings and gains similar positions of authority. Tea shops are nearly always successful enterprises, but only if with exertion amount of initial shock, undertake the starting of them."

"Touching on the day continuation schools, which come into existence with the New Year, will be an interesting career open to educated women."

"Labours works in village libraries is a splendid field that ro e opening to men and women. The salaries are about those given to women in similar occupations."

"Dress decorating can best be learned by girls who have great natural talent in the Court and stage decorating establishments. The pay received by a good dress decorator is very high, but a woman to succeed must have unusual talent and taste."

BIBLE PROBLEMS.

Answers to questions printed in the "Daily Express" on Saturday:—

117. i. Sam. 1, 17-29.   122. Amos 9, 3
118. i. Sam. 18, 27.   124. Lcth. 4, 7
119. 2. Chron. 24, 12.   2. i. and 8, 18
120. i. Kings 10, 22.   123. Exodus 31, 3
121. if. Kings 19, 14.   124. i. Sam. 7, 7-11
122. Acts 29, 3

(Copyright, 1920.)

Can You Cook Vegetables?

Vegetables are exceptionally good and cheap this season.

If housewives are taking full advantage of market condition by using more vegetables. The weekly prize of one guinea this week to be awarded for the best suitable for serving at lunch or dinner as a separate course. The recipes are to include addition to no more than six ingredients.

WOMAN'S DEPARTMENT,
"Daily Express,"
Shoe-lane, E.C.4.
Post not later than Wednesday morning.

For Smart Day
or
Evening Wear

Three-quarter Cape Coat of Black Velvet and Grey Fox, lined with grey and blue figured satin.

250 Prizes Every Week!

THE CHILDREN'S PAINTING COMPETITION.

Thousands of Little readers of the "Daily Express" will begin reading the adventures of the "Little Lost Bear" to-day.

Every week 250 splendid prizes will be given for the best painted or coloured drawings cut in by boys and girls between the age of two and fifteen.

The prizes will be divided into four classes:—

Class I.—Open to boys and girls of five and six years inclusive. 25 prizes.

Class II.—Open to boys and girls of seven to nine years inclusive. 75 prizes.

Class III.—Open to boys and girls of ten to twelve years inclusive. 75 prizes.

Class IV.—Open to boys and girls of thirteen to fifteen years inclusive. 75 prizes.

This picture, which should be cut out and coloured, may not be painted or cut out coloured. The only condition is that each coloured drawing shall be the same size as the original.

Do not send in your drawings yet. There will be clear directions in the "Daily Express" to-morrow telling all children what to do with the pictures they have coloured.

Little Lost Bear.   By MARY TOURTEL.

No. 1.—Mrs. Bear sends her little son Rupert to market.

Two jolly bears once lived in a wood.
Their little son lived there too.
One day his mother sent him off
The marketing to do.

She wanted honey, fruit, and eggs
And told him not to stray.
For many things might happen to
Small bears who lose the way.

Rupert and Mary

Rupert is an enduring fragment of childhood. It may come as something of shock to know just how old he really is, but it is true that there are septuagenarians alive who, when they were five years old, regarded him as one of their most precious friends, just as do many present-day children.

Rupert made his debut on 8 November 1920 in the pages of the *Daily Express* and has been a fixture ever since, albeit with occasional breaks of short duration in the early days. No feature in that newspaper has lived so long, and, for that matter, no other national newspaper in Britain has produced a character who has equalled Rupert in longevity. In the United States there has been a handful of comic strip characters who have actually lasted a great deal longer – the prime example being the Katzenjammer Kids, who made their debut in 1897, and lasted until the late Seventies.

But Rupert, strictly speaking, is not a comic strip, and the *Daily Express* does not like the word 'cartoon' either. What, then, is he? Officially a drawing, it seems. His appearance is normally limited to two frames

every weekday, advancing the story, each complete episode lasting on average for five weeks. During the war and immediate post-war period, when the shortage of newsprint severely curtailed the size of British newspapers, frustrated readers had to live with only one frame a day, and as a child who grew up in that period I can testify to the hardship such deprivation entailed, although, as I later discovered, that was the very form in which Rupert was launched back in 1920. Before the mid-Thirties his space could change drastically; sometimes he was in one large panel, sometimes in a row of four small drawings,

Opposite and right: Rupert, Britain's most famous bear, quietly makes his first appearance in the *Daily Express* on a Monday morning in November 1920, at the foot of the women's page.

Little Lost Bear.

BY MARY TOURTEL

No. 1.—Mrs. Bear sends her little son Rupert to market.

Two jolly bears once lived in a wood;
Their little son lived there too.
One day his mother sent him off
The marketing to do.

She wanted honey, fruit, and eggs,
And told him not to stray,
For many things might happen to
Small bears who lost the way.

Mary Tourtel – the creator of Rupert, and wife of the
newspaper's night news editor, Herbert Tourtel. It
wasn't simply a case of nepotism. When all attempts to
find an animal character that would enable the *Express*
to counter its Fleet Street rivals had failed, she came to
the rescue with the furry bear. A trained artist,
particularly skilled in the depiction of animals, she was
already established as an illustrator of children's
books. She was born in the cathedral city of
Canterbury, Kent in 1874 and died there in 1948.

and sometimes, even, merely a marginal ornamentation for a prose tale of his exploits.

Rupert underwent what was to prove his most significant change after 1935, the transformation effected by the taking over of the feature from its originator by Alfred Bestall. Only rarely does an illustrated character in a newspaper when it is passed on to other hands increase both its popular appeal and its quality, but that is what happened in this instance.

How then did Rupert start in the first place?

There has been, ever since children's comics came into existence in the latter part of the nineteenth century, a fondness for anthropomorphic characters, or animals who behaved as though they were humans. Anthropomorphism in literature is, of course, as old as

writing itself and through the centuries has provided a platform for humour and satire, as, for example, Aristophanes, Chaucer and Lewis Carroll have demonstrated. For the illustrator and cartoonist the attractions have been significant.

The league table of popularity has usually been led by bears, with mice probably coming a close second.

Bears, it would seem, have a good image. They are normally seen as lovable and furry. They do not come across as ferocious wild beasts and predators of the order of lions and tigers, although in reality they are easily as capable of inflicting similar damage to a human being unlucky enough to be in a position to be mauled. The bear is seen as a softer, altogether more amiable, ambling animal, but nevertheless possessed of a certain grandeur and strength. An artist may also feel that he can legitimately grant the bear a wider range of expression than most animals. They

The rivals of Rupert. The *Mirror's* Pip, Squeak and Wilfred were a craze in the Twenties, while the *Mail's* Teddy Tail became a formidable circulation builder.

Rupert and the Stolen Apples.

Mrs. Bear gives Rupert one fine day
Some apples ere he goes to play.

He takes his book beneath his arm
And decides to stroll to Hilltop Farm.

He sits beneath an apple tree
And reads and munches happily.

Little he thinks that watching him
Is a Policeman, stern and grim.

can often be seen to sport what may look suspiciously like a jovial grin and their eyes appear to twinkle. And young bear cubs are the most winsomely appealing animals of all – cuddly, wide-eyed, friendly and vulnerable, just waiting to be hugged.

Teddy bears began as a craze in America before the First World War and swiftly crossed the Atlantic. There never has been a more universal childhood mascot, and deprived indeed is the infant who has never possessed a teddy of his or her own. In short, the bear, with all its comforting cosiness, is a child's best non-human friend.

The British popular newspaper was almost certainly the invention of one man, Alfred Harmsworth, later Lord Northcliffe. It was he who first recognised that the vast new reading public, the fruits of the 1870 Education Act, which had made it compulsory for every young person to attend school, were waiting to be addressed, and that skilful marketing of a suitable product could win their loyalty. There had been a number of technological developments in newspaper production, which had sped up the printing process, and had made large print runs possible. Scarcely a corner of the British Isles lay outside the reach of a morning newspaper on the day of issue, thanks to the intricate, highly-developed railway system which was one of the great achievements of the Victorian era. In 1896 Harmsworth, already having published a number of other journals which had gained mass circulation, including *Chips* and *Comic Cuts*, the pioneers in the field of children's comics, launched the *Daily Mail*, which he billed as 'a penny newspaper for one halfpenny', and immediately scored a considerable success.

It also marked the beginning of modern Fleet Street. Other newspapers started up, including the *Daily Mirror* and the *Daily Express*. A pattern began to take shape that persists to this day. The *Express* was bought by an enterprising young Canadian who quickly made a public mark in Britain – Max Aitken, later Lord Beaverbrook – and he set out to beat the *Mail*.

Although newspaper strips had become established in America during the Nineties they took much longer to infiltrate the British press. This was partly due to the rapid development of children's comic weeklies, and the news stands were already loaded beyond saturation point with a multitude of titles long before the outbreak of the First World War. Many, however, were forced to close down as the war began to bite, and Northcliffe suddenly recognised that a gap in the market was opening up. Children may not have bought newspapers, but they could

Top: in early days there was no firmly established format for Rupert, and sometimes he was a strip, as here. Left: an early spin-off – a pop-up book, drawings by Mary Tourtel.

exert a certain amount of influence over their parents and would conceivably retain a loyalty towards their favourite newspaper when they reached adulthood. So children's sections began to creep in.

In April 1915 the first British newspaper comic strip was started, and directed at the child readership of the *Daily Mail*. It was called Teddy Tail, and drawn by Charles Folkard, a prominent illustrator of children's books. Teddy Tail was a mouse, and was given a large space in the paper, nine big panels each day, with captions, the stories running in serial form. It was an immediate success and there was already a Teddy Tail

An early Mary Tourtel story that was reprinted in book form and published in 1924.

book in the shops for Christmas of that year, the first of many to come. The character, Teddy Tail of the Daily Mail, apart from a six-year absence during the Second World War, was to run continuously in the newspaper until 1960.

Other managements eyed the *Mail's* success with envy, but were loath to start up a crippling circulation war while the real war was raging. Once it had ended it was a different matter, and newspapers quickly regained their pre-war size, in contrast to the situation prevailing after the Second World War. The *Daily Mirror*, in the spring of 1919, reopened its children's section, and launched a drawn panel featuring a dog and a penguin. Their names were Pip and Squeak. It went down

very well with the readers, and in a matter of weeks it had become a four-frame strip. Early in 1920 the unlikely couple found and adopted a baby rabbit, which they named Wilfred. The artist was A. B. Payne, a successor of Tom Browne, the creator in 1896 of Weary Willie and Tired Tim in *Chips*, one of the first British children's comics. He now became a famous and respected figure in Fleet Street.

Wilfred the rabbit was the most appealing of the three characters, with a vocabulary limited to the babyish gurgle 'Gug!', and 'Nunc', his way of saying 'Uncle'. All through the Twenties Pip, Squeak and Wilfred flourished, in strip form in the *Daily Mirror* and the *Sunday Pictorial*, as an annual and even in the form of animated films for the silent cinema. The Wilfredian League of Gugnuncs was formed, and raised many thousands of pounds for charity through its nationwide membership. A 1928 rally at the Royal Albert Hall was attended by nearly 90,000 people. Although it never regained the eminence it enjoyed in the Twenties, when it achieved craze status, the strip was brought back after an enforced wartime absence for the Saturday children's page, and continued until 1955, Payne remaining with it until almost the end.

Another daily newspaper, the *Daily News*, which later became the *News Chronicle*, produced a children's daily strip actually featuring a bear. The animal was called Happy and lived with a family of humans who appeared to be carved from wood. The Noah family had a menagerie of different animals, all generously endowed with various human traits, and naturally, their home was an ark. The Arkubs, as they were known, had been created by J. F. Horrabin, who simultaneously drew an adult strip about office life, called Dot and Carrie, in *The Star*, a London evening newspaper. The Arkubs, too, had a junior readership club, and its members were given badges proudly displaying their allegiance to the newspaper in which they appeared.

A PICTURE OF RUPERT FOR YOU TO PAINT

A Tourtel Rupert for colouring in. She preferred the sweater to be blue, the scarf grey.

The *Daily Express* watched their rivals' attempts to corner the children's end of the market, and realised that it would be necessary to compete with some anthropomorphic creation of their own. There was some dispute as to what form the creature should take, as the number of suitably furry animals had been diminished. There was a review of possibilities, but no conclusive ideas. The editor of the newspaper, R. D. Blumenfeld, was under instructions from the proprietor, Lord Beaverbrook, to find and launch a character that would eclipse those of the others, with particular venom reserved for the *Mail*, which then as now was looked on as the nearest Fleet Street enemy. None of the proposals seemed to fit the bill.

How Rupert actually came into existence is no longer easy to establish. The authorised version is that Blumenfeld confided in Herbert Tourtel, his night news eidtor, that he was having difficulty finding a suitable character. Tourtel's wife, Mary, was an animal lover, a classically-trained artist and a well-established illustrator of children's books.

14

Accordingly, Tourtel is alleged to have told Blumenfeld that he was sure that his wife could come up with something, and that she should make an attempt. Rupert was the result.

Peter Bessell, a former Liberal Member of Parliament now living in the United States, claims that Rupert was actually invented by his grandmother, who was a brilliant story-teller. One of the products of her imagination, Rupert and Margot, was sent to the *Express*, who were sufficiently impressed with it to pay her £50 for rights to use the characters. The legend had been passed down through his family, but documentary proof has not been found, as his grandmother's papers were destroyed in a fire. That there was a story called Rupert and Margot can be verified by looking through files of the newspaper, but it appeared after the launch of the Rupert character.

Mary Tourtel, or Caldwell, as she then was, was born in Canterbury, Kent, in 1874.

Her father, a stained glass artist and stone mason, worked on the Victorian restorations of the Cathedral. One of her brothers, Samuel, carried on the stained-glass tradition and worked for many years on the Cathedral windows, while her eldest brother, Edmund, became a celebrated animal painter in Africa, and a collection of his paintings is on display in Cape Town. Given such an artistic background it is unsurprising that Mary should have pursued a career in book illustration following her art school training. Her first publications, *A Horse Book* and *Three Little Foxes*, appeared in 1897, when she was 23, and shortly afterwards she married the squat, cigar-smoking Herbert Tourtel, then a sub-editor on the *Express*.

The couple were childless, and instead of raising a family seemed to spend much of their free time in extensive travel, an exacting experience in the days of steamships, when a voyage to Asia or Africa would have meant many weeks afloat. They went to Italy and

Rupert's frightened too
—how distant
seemed
The friendly coast to
him,
And Margot helpless,
with her he knew
So far he could not
swim.

Next moment they are in the sea.
Margot kept herself afloat
By clinging to the basket, while
Rupert looked round for a
boat.

None can he see, they're all alone,
For so it seemed to him.
What shall he do? Make for the
shore
And with Margot sink or swim?

splash! down they came. The air-
balloons
Have helped to break their fall
As the basket dropped upon the
sea;
They land safely after all.

✧   ✧   ✧

"Look!" Rupert said, "the
coast's not far."
He tells Margot he can swim
Should the basket sink, all will be
well
If she will trust to him.

The sea was calm, they kept
afloat.
But how long would they stay?
Meantime they thought it rather
fun
To float along this way.

✧   ✧   ✧

Alas! the basket proved a crazy
boat;
It began to settle down.
As it filled with water Margot
cried,
"Oh, Rupert! we shall drown!"

'Twas well for them two
fishermen,
Out with their nets
that day,
Seeing the basket fall
into the sea,
Wondered what had
come their way.

Tourtel verses enhanced the story, but rarely achieved literary merit, or even competence.

The Monster Rupert was an early Rupert annual, its cover showing the Tourtel colours for his clothes.

Egypt and India, and she filled pages of her ever-present sketchbook with detailed drawings of landscapes, people and animals. But as well as art and travel she had another, more surprising interest. She had an early fascination in flying and flying-machines, and was among the pioneers to go aloft as one of the first women aviators. The appearance of famous places from the air intrigued her, and is reflected in occasional unusual angles to be found in her landscapes. In 1919 she flew with her husband in a lumbering Handley-Page biplane on a record-breaking trip from Hounslow Heath to Brussels, a journey accomplished in 2 hours 35 minutes, foreshadowing the regular passenger services to be established in the Twenties from Croydon, the famous pre-war London airport, to various European capitals.

Thus it was that in 1920 her husband fulfilled a demanding executive role in the production of the newspaper, while she was an illustrator of some repute, specialising mainly in children's stories featuring animals. Prior to the first appearance of Rupert her work had already been seen in the pages of the *Express*, and consequently her talents were by no means unknown to the editor. In

the *Sunday Express* in 1919 she had been responsible for a feature called 'In Bobtail Land', which ran for six months, and at the same time she had produced 'When Animals Work' for the *Daily Express*.

Rupert's debut was unspectacular. There was the tiniest of announcements a few days earlier announcing that Mary Tourtel, 'a clever woman artist', had devised a story in pictures and verse, featuring an unnamed bear, but there was certainly no hint that the newspaper had found a character that would drive Teddy Tail and the others into the ground. Such a claim would in any case have been premature. At the foot of the women's page in the issue of Monday, 8 November 1920, there appeared a single panel drawing of a small bear with a shopping basket under his arm being sent by his long-skirted mother on a shopping errand, while in the doorway of their humble cottage the nonchalant father bear lolled with a hand in his pocket. The title above the story was 'The Little Lost Bear', while below was a short narrative in rhyming couplets setting up the plot, with underneath the promise that the story would be continued on the morrow.

Already, on his debut, the look of Rupert was established – scarf, sweater, check trousers, sturdy shoes. The trousers, it has to be said, look baggy by later standards, and he does also seem to have a thicker waistline, but even so it is unusual for the sartorial details to be settled on the very first day, and Mary Tourtel's Rupert of 1920 and the corresponding characterisation of 1985 are close enough in their appearance to be instantly recognisable as the same creature.

The first adventure, in which the little bear was lost in the woods near his home, meeting strange characters, before being reunited with his parents, was over in 36 episodes, finishing a few days before Christmas. The next story, Little Bear's Christmas, was all over in five days, an unusually short spell for Rupert, as it would turn out. In the initial stages there seemed to be little faith that the bear was going to be an enduring character,

De ridder rent door dichte bosschen,
Om zijne zuster te verlossen.

Als Bruintje komt in 't vreemde land,
Drukt Freddy Snuit hem warm de hand.

De poes wijst Beer de deur der schoone fee;
Gewis, nu brengt hij 't wonderkruid wel mee.

Door de woestijn, op een kameel gezeten,
Is Bruin spoedig huis en hof vergeten.

Zijn Beer en Snuit geen groote helden?
We mogen 't heusch wel eens vermelden.

De Snuit mag bij vriend Bruin logeeren;
Het tweetal zal zich amuseeren.

and there was no set pattern to his appearances. Sometimes he would only be a marginal figure illustrating a puzzle feature, or would be found in a prose story bereft of illustration. There were even times when he was altogether absent, the fort often being held by Mary Tourtel's other character, Margot. In the mid-Twenties he sometimes appeared in a four-frame story running across the foot of the page like a comic strip. The indecisive format could be attributed to difficulties Mary Tourtel had in meeting the inexorable deadline demanded by a regularly-appearing feature. Rupert's absence was often explained by an editor's note that the little bear was on holiday.

Mary Tourtel, for all of the unpredictability of the shape in which her stories would be told, at least was consistent in determining what kind of creature her creation should be. Rupert, although visibly a bear, was quite obviously a small boy, initially of a rather more furry appearance than later. His parents are big bears. His could be the ursine family into which Goldilocks made her inopportune foray, and Mary Tourtel was greatly influenced by fairy stories and nursery rhymes, which often provided her with both plot and imagery.

Some of the stock Rupert characters came on the scene at a very early stage. Algy Pug actually antedates Rupert himself, having been featured in a Tourtel story before November 1920. Bill Badger is another of the initial cast, and a close friend of the bear for 65 years. Edward Trunk, the elephant, also belongs to that select group of founding partners. The unremarked co-existence of human and non-human characters in the Rupert stories, always part of their charm, was established immediately by Mary Tourtel, with the appearance of the little girl Margot, to say nothing of the grotesque but humanoid ogres, dwarves and witches, and an array of kings, queens, princes and princesses together with their respective courts.

Rupert was popular in Holland even in the Twenties, and the postcard stories opposite and below, as well as the Dutch board game overleaf, first appeared at that time as early examples of Rupert merchandising.

Perhaps one of the most popular and enduring characters is the Wise Old Goat, a savant of mystic origin, whose presence sped many a yarn into the realms of the supernatural.

The animals are clothed and communicate easily to the humans in speech and, were it not for their facial features, are just like normal people. They are drawn in such a way that details of their anatomy are concealed. Rupert has an upright, human stance, making him a biped, and appears to have human hands instead of paws. His feet have been rarely seen, and on such occasion that his shoes are off, are concealed by the

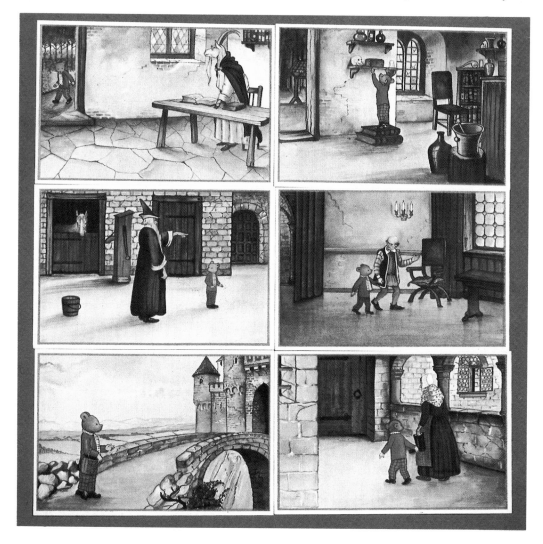

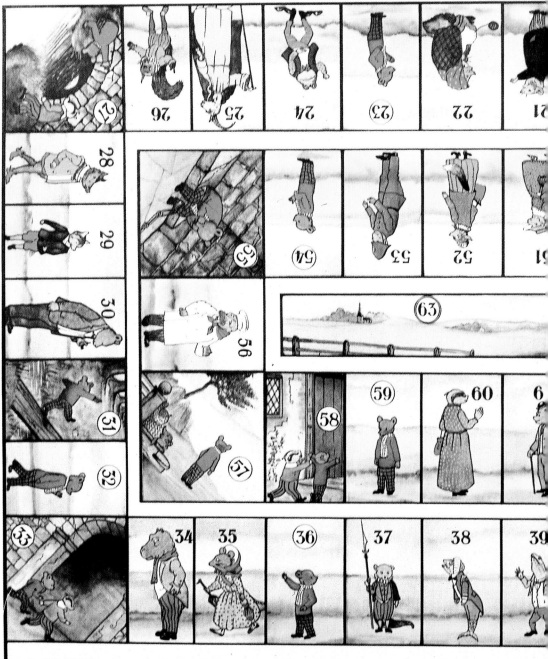

HET BRUINTJE BEER SPEL

De AVONTUREN van BRUINTJE BEER

De op dit spel voorkomende figuren zijn ontleend aan de in boekvorm verschenen serie verhalen. Deze boeken zijn verkrijgbaar bij ALGEMEEN HANDELSBLAD, N.Z. Voorburgwal 234-240, Amsterdam-C., de boekhandel en AKO- en Bruna-kiosken.

SPELREGELS

20

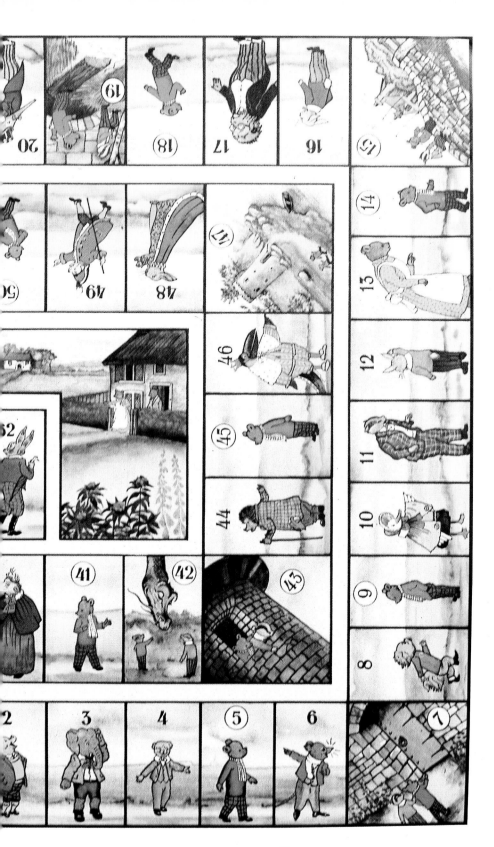

Opposite: the Rupert Little Bear series of books began to appear in 1925, to be followed in 1928 by the Little Bear Library with their famous yellow covers. Initially they were priced at one shilling (5p) but were later sold in Woolworth stores for sixpence, a bargain even then.

composition of the drawing. Occasionally, however, Mary Tourtel offered a totally unambiguous view of what unmistakably was a human foot.

Her imagination, particularly in the early years of Rupert, leaned heavily towards the magic elements of medieval fantasy, and there was an emphasis in her style towards sorcerers, enchanted castles, wizards, magicians, dragons, goblins, fairies and all the images to be found in the stories of Hans Christian Andersen and the brothers Grimm. Although Rupert's home in Nutwood was ordinary enough, and his immediate circle of friends, apart from possessing the heads of animals, as normal a collection of schoolboys as could be found anywhere, Rupert was a catalyst, the means whereby they could quickly find themselves plunged into amazing supernatural adventures in a kind of alternative world to the safe and cosy one they knew. Therein lay the secret of Rupert's popularity, the extraordinarily free range of his excursions into strange adventures. Mary Tourtel created wonderlands as vivid and meticulously detailed as Nutwood itself, and presented to the child readers of Rupert the idea that such parallel landscapes could exist right under the nose of her hero, who, it seemed, had only to take a stroll to run into strange characters and incidents which would whisk him off to such places.

Her style was scholarly and precise, and often exhibited a somewhat academic art school grounding. She was well versed in costume and decoration, and would invest her drawings with that knowledge, so that her courtiers and knights, princesses and beggarwomen, were authentically clothed, and her castles and places were correct in the application of architectural orders, sometimes with the meticulousness of a textbook. When she was on her best form one could be sure that a window or a halberd or a sword or a portcullis would be properly depicted, so much so that in a sense her drawings were often too good, too academic to serve as mere backgrounds for a child's adventure story involving an anthropomorphic bear.

Clearly, she had at her disposal an extensive visual reference library to which she frequently turned, and occasionally there are signs that such props were lacking, as background details become superficial, sketchy and even ill-defined. She also filled many sketchbooks with drawings of objects and animals, and took great pains to give her creatures accurate characteristics. Her painstaking figure drawing sometimes seemed to be accomplished at the expense of her compositions, which were usually meticulous but four-square. Very rarely did she select an unusual angle, and a sequence of her drawings could sometimes assume a certain monotony. Nevertheless, when viewed in the

context of competing work, Rupert was consistently superior in draughtsmanship. Payne's Pip, Squeak and Wilfred was by comparison slick and cartoonlike, and dashed out with a fraction of the draughtsmanship of Rupert.

Another persistent aspect of the Mary Tourtel Rupert is the virtually surrealistic juxtaposition of periods and situations. It is not uncommon in twentieth-century Nutwood to find people from the Middle Ages wandering around without attracting the faintest surprise from the present populace. Perhaps unconsciously she had hit upon one of the most attractive features of the Rupert stories – their timelessness. Nutwood is not only a place where time stands still – the village retains much the same sort of life it had in Mary Tourtel's day, a schoolhouse, a branch line railway station, a general shop, and Rupert and his

The Mary Tourtel yellow-covered Rupert books have been reprinted many times. These three volumes are the first from an edition produced in the mid-Seventies for sale through Woolworths.

friends still wear the boy's clothing of the Twenties.

The best Tourtel period was during the mid-Twenties, when she had hit her stride, and not begun to tire of her creation. Her plots, depending heavily on magic, developed imaginatively and often had elements of almost unbearable suspense. But with the passing of the years her storylines became somewhat elaborate and contrived.

There were problems in her private life. She suffered personal tragedy in 1931, when her husband, after a long illness which had required him to live abroad, died in a German sanitorium. He was 57, but totally burnt out. For much of Rupert's existence it was he who had supplied the verses accompanying his wife's drawings, which ranged from doggerel to quiet acceptable lines.

Without Herbert Bird Tourtel to oversee her stories, her style began to change. It is possible to detect a darker thread, and even the drawing style seems to be erratic. She was suffering from the strain of overwork, and repetitions of ideas became more frequent. Worse still, her eyesight was beginning to fail, making it increasingly difficult to fill her compositions with her characteristic fine detail.

Ironically, Rupert was more popular than ever. Many stories had been reprinted in book form, the first appearing from Thomas Nelson as early as 1921. Sampson Low began publishing compendiums of stories in 1924 under the generic heading of Rupert Little Bear Adventures, and in 1928 began the famous yellow-covered Little Bear series initially at 1/–, or 5p, a range of books which by the Thirties were only 6d, or 2.5p. Rupert also appeared in the *Daily Express Children's Annual* from 1930 onwards, but no plans had been laid at that time to devote an entire annual to the bear in his own right.

Just before Christmas 1932 the *Daily Express* Rupert League was formed. Considering that the Wilfredian League of Gugnuncs had ruled the roost throughout the Twenties, to the great advantage of the *Daily Mirror*, it is surprising that it took the *Express* so long to come out with a similar idea. The founder was the editor of the children's page, Stanley Marshall, who bore the designation 'Uncle Bill'. The aims of the League were high-minded, and members were obliged to respect their elders, assist the aged and the crippled, and be especially caring of very young children, while always maintaining a cheerful disposition. In those far-off innocent days such self-effacement was not considered eccentric, and the completed enrolment forms, sent off in return for three penny stamps, poured in, with the lucky members being sent an enamel badge by return.

At around the same time the *Daily Express* started a pull-out supplement in the paper, which although printed in broadsheet fashion, was folded into a tabloid size akin to a weekly comic. It was called the *Daily Express Children's Own*, and Rupert was given a prominent place in it. Unfortunately, Mary Tourtel was no longer capable of taking on the extra burden, and another artist had to be found. 'Uncle Bill' was not very successful; his chosen candidate, one Wasdale Brown, proved to be inept in making the familiar features of the bear even remotely recognisable to his public. In any case, the supplement was short-lived, and after a few lumbering issues quietly dropped.

What had been learned from this episode was that there would be a problem in replacing Mary Tourtel. The time was fast approaching when her health would force her to give up. By the middle of his second decade it was appreciated that Rupert was a valuable asset to the paper, and should be continued by someone else when his originator was no longer available. A quest began to find a successor, while arrangements were made to ease Mary Tourtel's retirement. She was given a pension and the book rights in many of her stories, which she passed on to Sampson Low in exchange for the steady royalties they would bring her for the rest of her life. For her last years she returned to Canterbury, and in 1948, aged 74, she died.

OUR SCRUM-HALF'S WIFE BUYS A MELON

By A. E. Bestall

2

Rupert meets Alfred

The moment has now come in which to introduce Alfred Edmeades Bestall. Among the many of potential successors to Mary Tourtel it was he who was chosen by the *Daily Express*. They had found him by casting the net far wider than the small circle of newspaper and weekly comic artists, none of whom, it seemed, was capable of continuing the Tourtel delicacy of line combined with robust story-telling.

In 1935 Alfred Bestall was an established illustrator, his work having appeared for many years in the superbly-printed, expensive social magazines such as *The Tatler* and *The Sketch* which were aimed at higher income readers. He had also been among the distinguished company of contributors to *Punch*, then, as now, a humorous weekly generally found in dentist's waiting rooms, but 50 years ago a more sedate vehicle of risibility than it has latterly become. A quiet bachelor in his early forties, he lived in a now-vanished form of residence, a boarding house for business gentlemen in Tavistock Square.

He was born in 1892 at Mandalay in Upper Burma, the son of a Methodist minister who had gone out there some years earlier as a missionary. Of the first four years of his life in the Far East he has no recollection, but a traumatic event occurred which left its mark on him for many subsequent years.

'Both my sister and I were brought home seriously injured in the upper spine and I have never found out how or why,' he says. At the time he was four, and his sister one. 'Her injury was much more serious than mine.' Did they fall off a pony, or fall down the stairs? Or was some dreadful crime committed by the

Pre-Rupert bears drawn by Alfred Bestall in 1930 illustrating a book, *Literary and Dramatic Readings*.

27

THE KING'S POCKET-KNIFE

Brownie Long-Beard is ushered out of the King's presence.

THE
PLAY'S THE
THING!

MUSICAL PLAYS
FOR CHILDREN
BY
ENID BLYTON

WITH MUSIC BY
ALEC ROWLEY
AND TWENTY-FOUR FULL PAGE DRAWINGS BY
ALFRED E. BESTALL

THE
HOME LIBRARY BOOK COMPANY
(GEORGE NEWNES LTD)
67 & 68 CHANDOS STREET W.C. 2.

Alfred Bestall's first endpapers, an illustration and the frontispiece from *The Play's the Thing*, a collection of plays for children by Enid Blyton, published as a lavishly produced special edition.

IN THE TOYSHOP

Clown

Teddy Bear

Fairy Doll

Doll
Golliwog

ayah who had them in her charge? 'I asked questions later, but my parents never told me. It could have been the pony – they had a contraption for children, a ring in which one sat which was somehow fastened on to the saddle. The only explanation I had a hint of was that I fell out of it on to my head.'

The accident, while not crippling him, left him with partial speech paralysis, and a persistent stutter.

'It gave me a hopeless outlook because I couldn't see how I could enter a profession if I couldn't speak properly.'

His handicap persisted until he was 45. 'I went to see a famous osteopath, who told me to sit down. He then went behind me, and gave me a fearful jerk, and I heard something click, and after more than forty years I was cured!'

As a child he was in the charge of another minister who had been in Burma before his father. He was brought up in Sheffield and North Shields, attending local schools. When his parents returned to England he was sent south to school at Southsea for a year. At the age of 12 he entered Rydal School, which was situated at Colwyn Bay on the northern coast of North Wales. The speech impediment did not affect his athletic capability, and he developed into a useful runner. He believes that his talent for drawing evolved from his inability to communicate vocally. The fluency which eluded him in speech came easily to his fingers.

By the time he was at Rydal he was drawing incessantly, filling sketchbooks with everything interesting that caught his eye. 'I should say that 19 times out of 20 when I was in trouble it would be for drawing on my exercise books when I ought to have been doing something else!'

During the period he spent there, Rydal, which had been founded only a few years

LOREL WAS ALL TANGLED UP WITH THE PERISCOPE

Above and left: the cover and a drawing from inside *The Spanish Goldfish*, a 1934 children's book illustrated by Alfred Bestall. Right: two double-page spreads from *The Tatler* in the Thirties. Overleaf: a humorous Bestall spread in *The Tatler* in 1925.

earlier, transformed itself from a small private establishment into a public school. Its centenary was celebrated in the summer of 1985. Alfred Bestall remained there until he was 18, leaving with his valuable matriculation certificate. The year was 1911.

'My top subject was geography, but I was passionately fond of ancient Greek. I wish that I had pursued geology as well. Art was an extra subject, and I did that, and if we staged school plays then I would do work for them. The staff all took it for granted that I would be an artist, much to their sorrow!

'From the time I was 16 I became tremendously enthused by the penwork that appeared in *Punch*. In those days *Punch* was the art gallery of British penwork – people like Partridge and Townsend, and Frank Reynolds. Ernest Shepard was just beginning. I sent up a drawing to them, but it came back with a note saying that the joke was altogether too feeble!'

On leaving school he went to live with his parents at Wolverhampton, for his father was

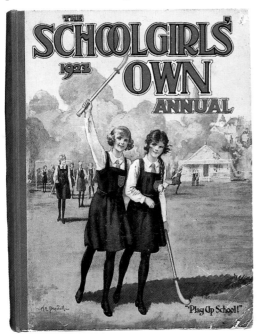

Alfred Bestall painted many covers for annuals published by The Amalgamated Press, such as this one for *Schoolgirls' Own*. Opposite: his humorous drawings, often featuring children, enlivened the pages of *Eve*.

by now in charge of the fine Methodist church there. He applied to the Wolverhampton School of Art, but was unhappy at the narrowness of the teaching to be found there at that time, and so instead sent a drawing which he had made on the spur of the moment, depicting a mouse's head in close-up, to the then Birmingham Central School of Art, the predecessor of today's college. It so impressed the admissions board that not only was he offered an immediate place, but also a scholarship to cover most of the costs of three years' tuition.

'My mother was also an artist, an experienced one, and she told me the three water colours to put together to get the most subtle shade of grey for the head. I was very pleased with it, and I sent it in and that was all I ever saw of it, because they kept it, but I got the scholarship!'

He left the Birmingham school in the summer of 1914, just as his father was transferring to a church in Surrey, and so he then arranged to continue his studies at the Central School of Art in London. The outbreak of war in early August of that year scotched such plans, and in common with hundreds of thousands of other young men he rushed to the recruiting office. 'For a whole year I was unable to get into the army. My chest was an inch short – in those days you had to have a full-size chest before they would allow you to go and get shot. Eventually, in October 1915, I applied at the Scotland Yard recruiting office off Whitehall, and they told me that in spite of my chest, I could have a go at six weeks in mechanical transport to see if I could put up with it.'

He was recruited into the Service Corps and marched off for basic training to a large camp that had been established in a park at Isleworth, on the western outskirts of London. Every morning his company was taken out in the charge of a bus driver, an employee of the London General Omnibus Company, the principal operator in the capital, and initiated into the mysteries of the legendary B-type engine and chassis. Many hundreds of

Elder Sister (startled): Did I hear you teaching baby bad words?
Gerald: Oh, no, Sis; I was just telling him some words he must never use!

Drawn by A. E. Bestall

B-types had been removed from the London streets and sent to France to be used as troop carriers, and in the early days of the war, before there had been time to repaint them in a drab military shade of khaki, homesick Tommies on their way to the front rode in red London buses still displaying advertisements for popular West End shows. Mechanically the B-type was a classic, a simple, rugged, efficient work-horse, and an early triumph of standardisation.

'I became extremely fond of the B-type, one of the easiest vehicles I have ever driven. Even changing gear was very easy, and of course we didn't have synchromesh then. On the Albion, on the other hand, which was chain-driven, it was very much harder to change.'

In January 1916 he was sent to France as a driver-mechanic, sailing the Channel from Southampton to Le Havre. He served his time in Flanders, in the 35th (Bantam) Division, which initially was meant to accommo-

date men below the general weight limit. By 1916 it had been opened up to full-size soldiers, who found themselves in the charge of bantam sergeant-majors, bantam NCOs, who, he recalls ruefully, wallowed in 'chucking their weight about.'

In the dreadful conditions of the forward areas trucks had a difficult time, and horses were still used near the front line, it being reasoned that they were more able to overcome the shell-pocked, muddy terrain. To the infantryman pinned down in the trenches the life of an army driver would have seemed like bliss, but Alfred Bestall was on many occasions under fire, and an easy target. Once in a large Thorneycroft, searching for a detached unit, he even found that he had strayed too far forward, and was confronted by a German machine gun with a crew of three, mounted in the middle of the road and aimed at him. After a momentary shock he realised that they were all dead.

When the war ended in 1918 he was at

Courtrai. 'We had heard that the end was coming, and then at eleven o'clock on the morning of November 11 we were suddenly aware of star shells being fired into the sky, in broad daylight, and the penny dropped – it was the end of the war. It was a slow business, coming home, because all the orders had to be revised, and so we sat for months in the channel ports. I wasn't demobilised until July 1919.'

He ended the war as he began, a private. He had been offered promotion to corporal, but it would have meant a desk job, and he had found that the open air life on the road had been beneficial for his health, and so turned down the offer.

'They soon found out that I was an artist. Drawing kept me occupied during the evenings, which could be deadly boring. I didn't drink at that time, and some of my friends would be in the bars getting so helpless that I

would have to frogmarch them back. They would ask me to do portraits of their girls from snapshots, so I made a lot of portraits. Even the officers would ask me to do portraits for them. Then Leslie Henson came out with a show for the troops, and after the armistice his group took over a theatre, and I did a page on it for *Blighty*, which in the First World War was issued free to the troops.'

His military service over, he returned to England for the first time since 1916, and went back to his parents' home, then in York Road, Woking, in Surrey.

'I was pretty sure what I wanted to do. At that time Fleet Street was full of humorous papers and magazines, stuffed with drawings, with captions underneath that were supposed to be funny, and these were an absolute godsend to me. James Mackenzie, who had been the editor of *Blighty*, asked me to call on him in Fleet Street because I had been sending him many humorous drawings from the army. When I went into his office he got up in

WHIPPED CREAM

(After A. A. Milne's " Rice Pudding")

What is the matter with Modern Girls ?
They're crazy on autos and lovers and pearls,
They've shortened their dresses and shingled their curls,
What *is* the matter with Modern Girls ?

What is the matter with Girl-of-To-day ?
Nobody stops her ; she has all her own way,
She frolics with life till it's all'antic hay ;
What *is* the matter with Girl-of-To-day ?

 What is the matter with Present-Day-Miss ?
 She's Freudian down to the most casual kiss,
 (Whipped cream and sweet pepper a strange diet is !)
 What *is* the matter with Present-Day-Miss !

  What is the matter with Modern Girls ?
  We've given them freedom, and politics, pearls,
  But they won't marry brokers if they can get earls,
  What *is* the matter with Modern Girls ?
        ETHEL MANNIN

a state of shock and stared at me. He then told me that I was the exact physical resemblance of his son, who had been killed in France. He shook my hand and wouldn't let it go. But he was enormously helpful to me in getting my work published.

In the competitive world of magazine illustration an artists' agent was a necessity, and Bestall became a client of Graham Hopkins, of the Byron agency, who became a close friend. The agent would not only visit all the major publications with samples of work, but would also be approached by publishers with commissions, which he would then pass on. There was a lucrative market in book publishing, since it was a prevailing fashion of the time for popular novels to contain line illustrations. One of the early assignments he fulfilled was a series of designs for costumes and scenery for an expensive presentation edition of Enid Blyton's plays for children, drawn in such a way that the ideas were simple enough for a schoolteacher to make herself. The volume also featured his first ever endpaper, drawn in pen and ink.

He began his painting with The Amalgamated Press, who published the *Girl's Own Annual*, a fat compendium of interesting juvenile matter, with colour plates. Working on these and on the covers of the annuals enabled him to break out from the restrictions of drawing largely in monochrome, either pen and ink or chalk.

An important target was *Punch*, which was regarded as a shop window for the best line illustrators. His first published drawing in 1922 depicted a skywriting aircraft outlining an advertising slogan in smoke. On the ground below a farmer's wife is summoning her husband, telling him that one of those new wireless messages had caught fire. Having sent it in he was surprised to be taken on by telephone, and asked to produce further work to a strict deadline.

'My association with *Punch* went on for

One of Ethel Mannin's parodies of A.A. Milne's verses, with decorations added by Bestall.

several years, but around 1932, at the time of the great slump, Frank Reynolds who was the art editor suddenly ceased accepting anything of mine. By that time I could draw without much trouble, you know. I'm always inclined to think that it was my own fault that Reynolds dropped me. I was doing a great deal of drawing before the slump. I was taken up by what we called the "big shinies" – *Tatler* gave me carte blanche through Graham Hopkins. They printed some of my large paintings over two pages. The principal thing in my drawing for *Tatler* was my ability to draw a pretty girl, preferably a society girl. Although I wasn't brought up in society I was able to do that sort of drawing.

'Frank Reynolds at that time was having a most unhappy life. His son had died and he himself was put into a hospital – it was such a shame because he was a brilliant man. The thrill of appearing in *Punch* before 1930 was a thrill I couldn't repeat.

'But I was doing such a lot after that, and consequently I wasn't really sending in so much to *Punch*.'

After retiring from his ministry, his father moved to Surbiton, but later went back out to Burma. Alfred Bestall, while going to his parents' house at weekends, settled in the hotel for gentlemen in Tavistock Square during the working week, and shared a studio with some other artists in Whitefriars Street.

'It was a whole floor of artists and I had my own room.' He rarely used live models, finding that he was able to get more vitality into his life drawing when he was merely relying on his imagination.

His versatility was extraordinary. In the prevailing tradition of the illustrators of the time he could turn his hand to virtually any subject. Some of his *Tatler* work, featuring lightly-clad young women in full colour, while mild by later standards, was pulse-quickening stuff in its day. There was a fashion for mounting verse within decorated pages containing vignettes of the subject matter, and he proved to be adept at producing atmospheric designs. Particularly effective

39

January 30, 1935]   PUNCH, *or The London Charivari*   113

Charivaria.

By means of electric welding (instead of riveting) the Bank of England is being rebuilt in complete silence. It is not believed that the further reconstitution advocated by Mr. Lloyd George could be effected so quietly.

⁎

"I do not write for personal profit," declares a novelist. Lots of other novelists have complained of much the same thing.

⁎

We are told that conscientiousness is the main factor that helps a man to gain promotion in his job. We have yet to hear, however, of the postman who was promoted for sticking to his post.

⁎

"Every man should carry his small change in a belt worn next to the body," says a magistrate. At present taxi-drivers seem to be the only persons who do this.

⁎

"No one could say that a converted barn is an ideal place in which to stay," writes a malcontent. We are afraid he has overlooked our house-agents.

⁎

One of our women gossip-writers had an aunt who looked like the Duke of Wellington. It would be interesting to know whether Mr. George Arliss as the Iron Duke has reminded her at all of the old lady.

⁎

Sir Ambrose Fleming observes that even an intelligent child reading the Genesis account of man's origin asks the question: "Who did Cain marry?"

An exceptionally intelligent child says "Whom."

⁎

In America two boxers knocked each other out simultaneously. We understand that the referee counted twenty over the two of them, but as neither got up he declared a draw.

"There, darling, you see we *are* going the right way."

"There are two Neville Chamberlains," says a politician. In the opinion of harassed taxpayers this is a terrible thought.

⁎

An Indian fakir is able to appear inside a house although all the doors and windows have been secured against him. No doubt he is inundated with offers from vacuum-cleaner manufacturers.

The Soviet executioner has been driven mad by overwork, and it is rumoured that his successor is to be allowed his Wednesday afternoons off.

⁎

Many complaints are still being received about the sediment in Post-Office ink. A man writes from Aberdeen to say that he has already ruined two fountain-pens.

⁎

Horse-skulls found in the walls of old churches are believed to be a survival of their use in temples of the Sacred Horse for oracular purposes. This throws a light on the origin of the expression "Straight from the horse's mouth."

⁎

In view of the difficulty of defining "loitering," might not a minimum speed-limit be imposed on users of pedestrian crossings?

⁎

"Young men in love often forget to stamp their love-letters," states a writer. The woman always pays.

⁎

A parachutist says that while dropping one has time to reflect upon the disappointments in life. And later one arrives at the sad conclusion that it's a hard world.

⁎

A news-item refers to a man who collided with a motor-cyclist and was hurled into a field of four-leaf clover. This is regarded as very lucky.

⁎

It is said that there are always Civil Servants sleeping at the Foreign Office. Even at night?

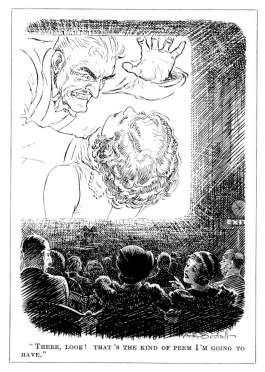

"THERE, LOOK! THAT'S THE KIND OF PERM I'M GOING TO HAVE."

Punch was a much sought-after platform for humorous illustrators, and Bestall's work appeared regularly between 1922 and 1935.

Mistress (interviewing new maid from the country). "... AND WHEN YOU ADDRESS ME I WISH YOU TO SAY 'YES, MUM,' OR 'NO, MUM.'"
Girl. "I COULDN'T 'ARDLY DO THAT—MOTHER MIGHTN'T LIKE IT—BUT I'LL CALL YOU 'AUNTIE' IF YOU LIKE."

were his illustrations for a series of A. A. Milne parodies by Ethel Mannin. He was also a painstaking composer of humorous drawings, either in line or wash, and much of his best work frequently featured children. It was the heyday for this type of illustration, and superb printing techniques ensured excellent reproduction. He also illustrated historic and romantic fiction, and was a well-known contributor to educational books.

In 1935 the call came for him to go to see the *Daily Express*, then engaged in the increasingly desperate search to find a suitable successor for Mary Tourtel. 'I knew Rupert, but I hadn't followed it particularly carefully. When the call came I thought that as it was something I hadn't tried before, I might as well have a shot at it, and I drew a few scenes with Rupert in them.

'When I wasn't staying with my people in Surbiton I lived in Tavistock Square, and I used to enjoy walking down from there, via

Red Lion Street on various short cuts to Fleet Street. And after a time I noticed that I was often walking either in front of or just behind somebody else from this same hotel for men. And one day I asked him if he was interested in Fleet Street, and he said yes, he had always been in publishing, but he hedged about what his specific line was.

'I sent my Rupert drawings in and was immediately asked to go in and see them. There were six people there as I walked in, and I sat down in front of them as my drawings were passed among them, and to my astonishment I saw that one of the group was the man I had been walking to Fleet Street with, and he indicated to me to keep quiet about it! The drawings went back and forth, I don't think any of them knew what to say – in fact there was one man who said absolutely nothing throughout and I afterwards learned that he was Arthur Christiansen, the editor. Anyway, finally the features editor said that they had decided to ask me to draw a Rupert story, and told me how much I would get, which wasn't much. I accepted but shocked them by saying that I would have to have the story at once as there wasn't much time, since the current and last Mary Tourtel story was already in the paper.

'They all looked alarmed, so I said if you let me construct this story and it turns out satisfactorily will you supply any subsequent stories? They hastily agreed, shook hands and walked out, all excepting the man I knew, who turned out to be "Uncle Bill". Beaverbrook had spotted him working on a newspaper in the north, and had brought him in to start the Rupert League. The Rupert League had been very successful in building circulation, but had begun to cost too much to run, and by now the *Express* was confident enough to be able to stop it, which they did, just as I joined. But "Uncle Bill" or Stanley Marshall, his real name, was given the task of finding Mary Tourtel's successor, and was delighted that it was going to be possible for me to do it.

'He took me on one side and said that whatever I did with it I must try to keep off fairies. It seemed that Mary Tourtel, whenever she had got Rupert into a jam and couldn't get him home again, would introduce a fairy to wave a magic wand. Believe it or not, the children wouldn't accept it, they thought that it was silly. The other thing she had been doing was introducing a few horrific characters that were giving children bad dreams, and there had been complaints from parents. I had to try to follow these orders!'

'But the promised subsequent stories never came. I had to do them all.'

Alfred Bestall never met Mary Tourtel, and indeed only ever saw one photograph of her. Certainly there was no consultation on the ground rules for depicting the character.

Assisted by a generous pension from the *Daily Express*, and the royalties from the Little Bear Library, the small yellow books which enjoyed considerable sales throughout the Thirties, she had retired to Llandrindod Wells, a genteel Welsh town renowned for its medicinal springs, where in spite of her poor eyesight she was able to go for long country walks. Her last Rupert story published in the newspaper, and sent in from Wales, was 'Rupert and Bill's Seaside Holiday', which ended on 27 June 1935. A few years before she died she returned to Canterbury.

There was little time for Bestall to work himself in. An editorial decision had been made to feature Rupert in two drawings each morning, rather than the larger single panel generally preferred by Mary Tourtel. The drawing was intended to illustrate the 80 words of narrative appearing beneath, and while he found it thrilling to produce a story in this format, he also found that it was extremely hard at first to meet the exacting deadline that had been set. Every other commission had to be dropped in order to serve Rupert. After the roughs in pencil had been approved by Stanley Marshall, the final drawings were made in pen and ink, and the first Bestall story, 'Rupert, Algy and the Smugglers', began to appear in the paper even as its artist was only three weeks ahead of it in planning what was to be a tale spread over 54 days.

He had submitted a narrative account of the story, and to his amazement found that his words were set in type to run underneath the pictures. The rhyming couplets were dispensed with, at least in the pages of the newspaper. Having seen that his hasty prose was to be immortalised he realised that he would have to take more care with it, and henceforth would devote as much attention to the words as to the drawing itself.

It did not take him very long to hit his stride, and soon it was apparent to readers that their beloved Rupert was being presented to them with much more confidence and verve. The most immediately noticeable effect of the change was that the storylines

TEXT CONTINUES ON PAGE 63

Rupert's Autumn Adventure **was the second Bestall Rupert story to appear in the** *Daily Express***, from August to October 1935, and it featured in the first Annual in the following year, and again in 1983, in full colour.**

"It's time to clear the apple trees.
So, Rupert, come and help me, please."

He gets the baskets out with pride.
And Daddy lets him have a ride.

Then Barbara's Grandma passes by.
Thoughts of her garden make her sigh.

But Rupert hears her sigh and asks
If he may do her garden tasks.

"I'll come and help you, Granny! See,
I've even brought my rake with me!"

When Barbara sees he's brought his rake
She cries, "A bonfire's what we'll make."

So busily they rake and sweep
'Til all the leaves are in a heap.

When Granny's safely lit the fire
They watch the blaze leap higher and higher.

"Let's get some more leaves," Barbara cries,
"To feed the fire before it dies."

They go to fetch the leaves and see
Two curious footprints by a tree.

Another footprint Rupert sees,
Then Granny calls out, "Teatime, please!"

To leave off searching seems a shame.
It's really an exciting game.

The wireless news at six o'clock
Gives all the Bears a nasty shock.

"Barbara is missing from her home.
She's not the sort of child to roam."

Now Rupert knows what he must do.
Those footprints may provide a clue.

Yes, when he gets back to the spot,
Of Barbara's prints he finds a lot.

So through the hedge he crawls and sees
The prints go on among the trees.

They lead him to a forest black
Where fallen leaves conceal the track.

And there he hears a wise owl cry,
"Some time ago a child passed by."

He searches for her all around
And finds her hanky on the ground.

He gets to where the trail divides.
"She turned for home here," he decides.

He hurries on and soon he sees
Her fast asleep beneath the trees.

She cries, "But how shall we get back?"
He says, "The footprints make a track."

When darkness hides the track from sight
They know they'll have to stay the night.

Says Rupert, "You sleep in this tree
And leave the lookout job to me."

So Barbara, free from worry, sleeps
And Rupert lonely lookout keeps.

At dawn he thinks, "To rest I'll try."
But hears a crashing noise nearby.

And then he hears a woodman shout,
"You're trespassing. Come on, clear out!"

Poor Barbara starts up in alarm.
The woodman grabs her by the arm.

Says Rupert as they're led away,
"We lost our way and had to stay."

A flying shape the man's hat grasps.
He lets them go. "What's this?" he gasps.

The chums, so suddenly set free,
Grasp at the chance to turn and flee.

"More footprints! Look here on the ground.
Exactly like the ones we found."

Then Barbara whispers, "Look at that!
That man there has the woodman's hat."

"I'll gladly help you if I can,"
He says. "My master hates that man."

"More leaves" he says. "I need a stack.
If you help me I'll lead you back."

The basket's full. The job is done.
"A ride," the servant says, "you've won."

They set off balanced on his head,
Then meet the man from whom they fled.

As Rupert thinks, "What will he do?"
The servant shouts, "Hold on, you two!"

High in the air the servant shoots.
"Aha!" he says, "I've spring-heeled boots."

Though over streams and woods he leaps,
The servant in a straight line keeps.

"That's where we're bound, yon castle fair.
Just one more leap and we'll be there."

A strange old man the chums now meet.
He says, "Please do come in and eat."

The table's bare. They wonder why.
Switches and bulbs catch Rupert's eye.

His breakfast plans amaze the chums.
A switch is touched and down it comes.

"These plates are real gold!" Rupert cries.
"I make that gold," the man replies.

"Now to my workshop follow me.
Here I make gold from plants, you see."

"Pour in the leaves, please," says the man.
"Watch! Gold will drop into that pan."

"We're off to find some leaves most rare.
Please guard my castle, Rupert Bear."

Still wondering at what they've been told,
The helpful chums bag up the gold.

A banging interrupts the chums.
They wonder, "Who is this who comes?"

They open up and see too late
That it's the woodman with a mate.

They threaten Rupert: "Come on show
Us where's the gold!" But he says, "No!"

They find and take it, they've no shame.
The chums think, "We shall get the blame."

But Rupert's thinking of a plan
To beat the baddies if he can.

He jumps aboard a moving stair
He'll signal from the roof up there.

"Oh, help us! Help us!" Rupert cries.
But all in vain. No one replies.

The men growl, "In you get, you two!"
They don't see Barbara drop a clue.

The servant storms. The chums he blames
"I'm sure you're wrong," the man exclaims.

Beside the cart tracks they soon find
The hanky Barbara left behind.

For miles the chums are driven fast,
And by some high rocks stop at last.

A sentry guards the gang's stronghold.
"Captives!" he's told. "As well as gold?"

The gang's chief says, "All will be well
If you that old man's secret tell."

"I won't!" says Rupert, so they're shut
Inside a dark and dirty hut.

Next day for food they're told to look
And give it to the bandits' cook.

Some mushrooms presently they find.
"No!" cries a rabbit. "Poison! Mind!"

He also says, "Take my advice.
Up there are berries, really nice."

They hear a plane and scan the skies.
"A rescue party!" Rupert cries.

So Rupert's scarf is wildly waived.
But from these rocks can they be saved?

The plane flies off. They're near to tears.
And then a parachute appears.

"Come on!" says Rupert. "Don't just stand!
We've got to see where it will land."

A parcel to the 'chute is tied.
"Let's open it," the chums decide.

They open up. They gasp. They stare.
The servant's spring-heeled boots are there!

"Now you can fly for help in these.
But first you better try them, please."

His practice causes lots of fun.
He bounces when he tries to run.

Then right into a tree he shoots.
But soon he can control the boots.

"Now," Rupert says, "don't be afraid.
I'll soon be back with lots of aid."

Above the bandits' heads he springs.
Amazed they cry, "He must have wings!"

He leaps clear of the sentry bold.
He'll save both Barbara and the gold.

Then when at last he is quite free,
To find his way he asks a bee.

So rapid and so straight its flight.
It's hard to keep the bee in sight.

A lake it crosses, wide and deep.
Though, tired now, Rupert tries to leap.

Alas, his leap is much too short.
And in the swampy mud he's caught.

He grabs an overhanging tree.
The boots stay stuck. But he gets free.

The bee no longer can be found,
So Rupert climbs to look around.

From here the castle he can see,
And to the servant shouts, "It's me!"

The servant cries, "Oh sir, I fear,
The little bear's got stuck near here."

"I'm glad you've come," cries Rupert Bear.
"Your boots are in the mud down there."

The servant crawls along the plank
And brings the boots back to the bank.

The plank is propped against the tree.
"Now here I come!" cries Rupert. "Wheee!"

The servant dons the boots and bounds
With Rupert to the castle grounds.

Soon Rupert's story has been told
Of how the baddies stole the gold.

They fly 'til in the twilight glow
They see the bandits' camp below.

So Rupert and his little friend
By powerful parachute descend.

Soon near the blackberries they land,
And hurry forward hand in hand.

To Barbara's hut they make their way.
"We've come to take you home," they say.

Beside the gold the sentry sleeps.
To rescue it the servant creeps.

They get the gold then off they fly.
To hide 'til morning they must try.

At dawn they see the plane appear.
There's something on it looks most queer.

The servant says, "Now in you climb."
"The men!" cries Barbara. "We've no time!"

They jump in. Rupert cries, "What sport!"
The servant, though, is almost caught.

The basket's swung up in the air.
The bandits shake their fists and glare.

When Rupert wonders how they'll land,
His friend climbs up hand over hand.

Up to the plane the line's hauled in.
"I say!" cries Rupert. "What a din!"

61

The old man says, "Before we reach
Your village, here's a present each."

And then by parachute the pair
Come floating homeward through the air.

Laughs Mr. Bear as down they spin,
"How good of you pair to drop in!"

Then Granny comes and soon they've told
Of how they won their gifts of gold.

were stronger, more capably worked out, with proper logical progressions. The easy 'with-one-bound-Rupert-was-free' approach of Mary Tourtel, in which she would invoke sorcery to extricate Rupert from difficult situations, was replaced by ingenious, and often humorous narrative sequences.

The most exciting innovation came a year after the Bestall takeover. Marshall declared that there were enough adventures that had appeared in the paper to collect them all together in one volume and make an annual out of it. Some doubters, including Alfred Bestall himself, felt that the stories had appeared too recently to appeal much to their regular readers in book form, since any reg-

ular reader would know their outcomes, and some young enthusiasts even made their own Rupert books by cutting out the daily frames and pasting them in their own scrapbooks. In those years preceding the Second World War, under the editorship of Arthur Christiansen, the *Daily Express* allocated a generous daily space to Rupert and the drawings were well displayed, so it was possible for the block-maker to get the most value out of the carefully-wrought details. For the Annuals the addition of a second colour was budgeted, and graduations of salmon pink were laid over the familiar black-and-white drawings. In the autumn of 1936 *The New Adventures of Rupert* was published, which contained five

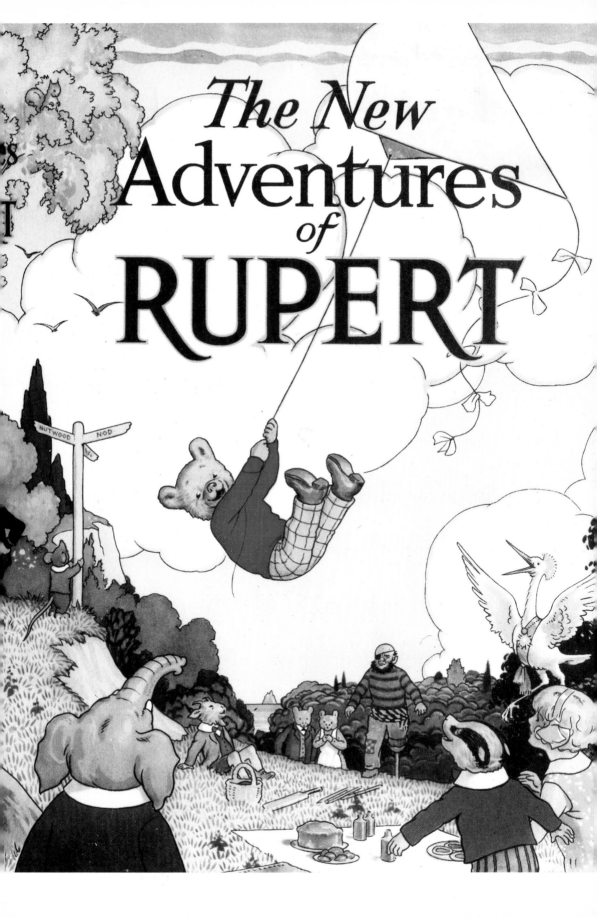

The New
Adventures
of
RUPERT

How the colour is applied to the Rupert Annual. Alfred Joll of Greycaines was responsible for bringing colour to these books, and in the early days it was achieved with a build-up of colour stipples, or dots, mechanically applied by plate artists. The technique adopted from 1979 is shown above. In the top left is the original pen-and-ink drawing by Bestall. It is mechanically copied in light blue, which is invisible to the reproduction camera. Bottom left: the 'blue' drawing is hand coloured by an artist – Doris Campbell is the most prominent. The original line drawing is then overlaid to produce the final result, as the reader sees it, bottom right.

complete stories – 'Rupert and the Wonderful Kite'; 'Rupert, Algy and the Cannibals'; 'Rupert's Autumn Adventure'; 'Rupert, Bill and the Pearls'; 'Rupert's Christmas Adventure'. The dust jacket, echoing the theme of the first story, showed Rupert with his kite.

The verses, so much part of the Mary Tourtel Rupert, were revived to run under each picture, four to a page, while a text narrative covered the same ground in prose. Bestall wrote the narrative but the sometimes banal couplets were the work of others.

The Annual was an enormous success, much to the chagrin of Sampson Low, who ceased issuing any more of the little yellow books after its appearance. A large number of them remained in print, and some years later many of the titles in the series were republished in new editions. But the popularity of the Annual, in spite of the fact that the stories in it had only recently appeared in the newspaper, undoubtedly hit sales of the Mary Tourtel books badly. In succeeding years it became possible to gather the stories from a longer time period, lessening the degree of over-familiarity, and also from 1940 onwards full-colour reproduction was introduced. Alfred Bestall did not undertake this work, confining his Rupert colouring to the cover painting, and later to the endpapers. The black-and-white illustrations for the stories nowadays are photographed as pale blue keylines which the colourist then works on, using muted pastel shades. Then an overlay of the original drawing in black line is applied, and the result is usually aesthetically pleasing and greatly superior to the prevailing standard of children's illustration. Until 1979 the overlays were produced by tracing the originals on to glass (later film) and the colour underlay by transferring the tracing on to Whitman paper.

With the Annuals the familiar red sweater and yellow check scarf and trousers became standardised. Mary Tourtel, with her covers for The Monster Rupert, a series of large format books published by Sampson Low between 1931 and 1950, preferred to depict Rupert with a blue sweater and grey check trousers, but there was no doubt which was now regarded as the *correct* form.

By some curious quirk, while Rupert in his adventures always had a white face, the covers of the Annual showed him with a brown face. This inconsistency stemmed from Mary Tourtel's habit of giving him a brown head on her covers, although her bear was much huskier and browner than the Bestall version. An attempt in the Seventies to upset this tradition proved to be disastrous.

Although on the one hand the appearance of the Annuals was immensely improved with the introduction of colour to the stories at the instigation of Arthur Joll of Greycaines, the printing company, on the other there was an enforced reduction in pagination and the compulsory adoption of a paperback format following the onset of the Second World War. There was no board available for the covers between 1942 and 1949.

Wartime seriously affected Rupert's daily newspaper appearance as well. Newsprint rationing became increasingly severe, and eventually broadsheet newspapers such as the *Express* were reduced to a single sheet. From 16 April 1940 there was room for only one, much smaller Rupert drawing each day, and it was not until 1949 that the two-frame format was restored, although never again in the generous pre-war proportions.

That Rupert survived at all during the war was due to the determination of the newspaper's proprietor, Lord Beaverbrook, who felt that to remove him would be damaging to the national morale. His rivals, such as Teddy Tail and Pip, Squeak and Wilfred had been swept away, allowing more precious space to be devoted to reporting the progress of the war. But Rupert clung on tenaciously at the foot of page 2, which had become the leader page, and was squeezed out by events on only two crucial days of 1940, when the fate of Britain hung in the balance.

But the world of Nutwood continued as it always had, unmarred by cataclysmic topical events, and apart from a reference to a villain who could possibly be a spy, there was no blackout there, no rationing and certainly no uniformed troops in armoured vehicles hurtling down the narrow lanes. Rupert endured, symbolising the continuity of normal life in a world that seemed to have gone crazy.

Although approaching fifty Alfred Bestall, as well as drawing Rupert, 'did his bit' for the war effort, serving as an air raid warden in Surbiton, where he lived in Cranes Park. During the V1 attacks of 1944 the southwest London suburbs were directly in their path, and it was no sinecure being an ARP warden. A painting he made of the wardens' post at the foot of Surbiton Hill hangs on the wall of his cottage in Wales as a reminder of that tiring and turbulent period.

RUPERT'S BALLOON PUZZLE

"There's the balloon man," says Rupert, "and, look, the wind has blown his balloons into a circle. I wish I had money to buy one."

"Never mind about money," says the man, "I'll give one free to the first of you who can solve this little puzzle: Pretend you are going around that circle in the same direction as the hands of a clock. Take away one balloon, then pass over two balloons and take away the third one, then pass over two more and take away the third again, and so on, round and round, until you have only two balloons left. Now, which balloon must you start with if the last two left are both to be blue ones?"

The pals think carefully. "I should start with the purple one," says Bill Badger. "No, the dark red one," says Rupert. "I should say it's the green one," murmurs Willie the mouse. "And *I* think it's the orange one," says Pong Ping.

(Does any one of the little people win a free balloon? Try it with eight pieces of paper.)

3

Alfred and The Annuals

Initially, when he took over Rupert, Alfred Bestall had hoped to be able to carry on his other work at the same time, but quickly found that it was a full time job. He had made a rod for his own back because he put so much skill and effort into a single frame, and it would take him at least half a day to produce it. Given that he had to provide perhaps a dozen illustrations a week, although that number was later halved in wartime, and that he also drew sundry other items for the Annuals, such as titles and other page decorations, puzzles, special features and the cover, as well as from 1944 original stories that were only to appear in the Annual, and were never published in the newspaper, there was scarcely enough time for him to keep up with the bear, let alone take on other commissions. Nevertheless, from 1935 until after the war he toiled on without any increase in his fees from the paper.

His pay was for the most part 12 guineas a week, or £12.60 in modern currency, calculated on the basis of a guinea a drawing, in 1935 a respectable weekly income. Later it was raised to 18 guineas.

'I never regarded it as a moneyspinner,' he says, 'but it took a long time to get any more money, in spite of Lord Beaverbrook saying that Rupert was the best children's character

in any newspaper anywhere in the world.'

It was his ideal to get three months ahead with his drawings so that there would be a well-stocked bank of them in hand should it become necessary for him to take a rest. Although the arrangement meant having to work on the Christmas story in the heat of July, it did not perturb him.

However, three years after the end of the war a thrusting new marketing executive, Albert Asher, responsible for a number of successful promotions, turned his attention to Rupert, and instigated a series of Rupert tales in quarterly book form, the Adventure series. It was a period in which the newspaper pursued an aggressive stance in relation to its rivals in the rest of Fleet Street, building up its circulation to become the front-runner. Beaverbrook was determined that the *Daily Express* should tower above its rivals, and be in the best position to garner the fruits of the expected boom in advertising that would occur once the austerity of the immediate postwar period was over. Asher was responsible for publicity-attracting promotional schemes such as a round-Britain yacht race. His brashness did not make him universally popular, and when he turned his attention to the children's editor he became the bane of Stanley Marshall's existence. Bestall believes that it was stress brought about by Asher's

heavy-handed interferences that hastened the heart attacks which were to end Marshall's life.

Gamely, Bestall took on the Adventure series, and supplied original stories for them in addition to his work on the Annuals and the daily newspaper. But the extent of the task caused him to overwork and he became ill. As he was now approaching his sixties he was advised by his family doctor to drop Rupert altogether and retire.

Bestall explained to the executives of the newspaper the dilemma he faced, and told them that it would be impossible for him to continue with the Adventure series. He discovered that there was a failure to appreciate just how intensive and difficult his input was, largely because the accomplished fluency of his line somehow gave a misleading impression that it was all very easy. With considerable reluctance on their part, as they were loath to lose his services, it was agreed that someone else would have to be brought in to work on Adventure original stories. They found an artist called Alex Cubie, and

Above: two titles in the postwar Adventure series, first published in 1948 and 1950. Right: two Bestall endpapers from Annuals.

instructed him to spend six weeks studying and practising the Rupert style.

'At first he was out of his depth,' said Bestall, 'so far from the Rupert that I had been doing, that we had to look around for someone else, and we found a lady called Enid Ash, whose work was good, especially with animals, except that she couldn't do Rupert's face. So we reached a compromise – somebody else did the stories, she would do everything else in the drawings, and I would put in the heads and faces of Rupert and all his pals, and so we carried on.'

Until this time he had been producing Rupert without any pause for fifteen years. The 1950 Annual returned to the hardback format, and it was felt that decorative endpapers would enhance its appearance, a challenge that he was happy to accept, particularly since he had been told that he could retain the artwork during his lifetime as his

TEXT CONTINUES ON PAGE 90

RUPERT

*"That's Pong Ping sitting over there.
And crying, too!" says Rupert Bear.*

Rupert is strolling through a field nea[r]
Nutwood one day when he spies his chum Pon[g]
Ping, the little Peke, sitting on a fence, looking ver[y]
glum. As he gets nearer he sees that Pong Ping ha[s]
been crying, which is not like him. "I say, what'[s]
up?" Rupert asks. "Oh, I'm so very homesick,[]"
the Peke sniffs. "But *this* is your home," says Ruper[t.]
"Not always," replies Pong Ping. "Climb up her[e]
and I'll explain."

and PONG PING

"*Why, what's the matter?*" *Rupert cries.*
"*I'm homesick,*" *poor Pong Ping replies.*

Pong Ping's medallion makes him ache
A journey to his home to take.

"I was born in a far-off land where my father was the Emperor's favourite," Pong Ping begins and at the same time produces a medallion. "The Emperor gave him this badge and I wear it in memory of him. How I wish I could go back for a visit." "It *is* difficult, isn't it," Rupert murmurs. Then he has an idea. "Let's ask the Professor!" he exclaims. And a moment later the chums are hurrying towards their old friend's tower house.

"*The old Professor's sure to know*
Some way or other you may go!"

RUPERT'S FRIEND MAKES A CALL

"This medal's from too far away
For me to send you, I must say."

"My radio room is close at hand.
We'll try to speak to that far land."

The old man twirls the knobs around,
And presently they hear a sound

Alas, the words don't mean a thing.
"I'll understand them," cries Pong Ping.

"First we must find out where your far-off land is," the Professor says when he hears Pong Ping's problem. "Your medal may give us a clue." And he studies the medallion closely then takes down book after book and pores through them. "Got it!" he cries at last. "This medal comes from a land deep in the Far, Far East. I can't *send* you there. But perhaps I can get a message through for you." Next moment Rupert and Pong Ping find themselves in the Professor's very own radio room.

The chums have never seen anything like it, and they gaze, open-mouthed, as the Professor twiddles and tunes and turns knobs and dials. At last he nods and puts on a pair of earphones. "Nutwood calling!" he repeats into the microphone then listens hard. He frowns and shakes his head. "I've got through, all right. But I can't understand a word they're saying." "Let me try!" Pong Ping cries. "I speak the language of that country." And the Peke jumps up and down in excitement.

RUPERT KEEPS A LOOKOUT

So Pong Ping stands upon a chair
And listens in with special care.

"The Emperor spoke!" he cries with glee,
"And said, 'Please come and stay with me'."

They think the Emperor's sure to send
His fastest 'plane to fetch his friend.

So Rupert watches from a crag
While Pong Ping goes to pack his bag.

At once the Professor gives Pong Ping the ear-phones and stands him on a chair in front of the microphone. Rupert watches his friend getting more and more excited as by turn he listens and talks in a language that the little bear does not understand. When Pong Ping at last jumps down from the chair he does a little dance of joy. "I've spoken to the Emperor himself," he shouts in glee. "And what do you think? He's going to send for me to go on a visit to him!"

The two chums thank the old Professor for his help and dash excitedly back to Nutwood. "The Emperor didn't say how he was going to send for me," pants Pong Ping, "but for such a long journey it surely must be by airplane!" Rupert is happy for his pal and he says, "You go and pack your things and I'll keep watch." Rupert hurries home, explains what is happening, begs some sandwiches and lemonade from Mrs. Bear then makes his way to a hillside that faces east and starts his lookout.

RUPERT GETS A SCARE

One day while Rupert's looking out,
The hill begins to shake about.

The trees shake too, the squirrels flee,
And Rupert runs, fast as can be.

And then there bursts with frightful sound,
A metal monster through the ground.

Frightened, poor Rupert runs to hide,
As from the monster two men stride.

Rupert waits and watches all afternoon but there is no sign of any airplane. Next day and the day after that, he and Pong Ping take turns at keeping watch. Then just when Rupert thinks nothing is ever going to appear, the hillside starts to shake. As rocks begin to fall Rupert jumps up and dashes towards home. To his horror the earthquake seems to be everywhere and he sees little animals fleeing in terror. "This is awful," pants poor Rupert as he runs. "What can be happening?"

Every second the earthquake gets worse with the ground shaking and trembling. Then the ground just behind Rupert heaves and pitches him on to his face. Thoroughly frightened, he scrambles behind a rock and looks back. And gasps! For, from a hole in the earth has crawled out the most strange machine. It has great claw wheels and a spinning nose for boring through the earth. Then to his amazement, a door opens and two foreign-looking men climb out.

RUPERT FETCHES PONG PING

Around their necks hang shiny things;
Medallions just like Pong Ping's.

"You're from the Emperor!" Rupert cries.
"I'll fetch Pong Ping", and off he flies.

"Your friends," shouts Rupert to his chum,
"By some strange kind of tank have come!"

Then off to greet them Pong Ping hies.
"So glad to see you, friends!" he cries.

Hoping he has not been spotted, Rupert hides behind a tree. But the two strangers have seen him and run straight to where he is hiding. At once they start to talk very fast. Poor Rupert can't understand a word they say, then all at once he spots that both are wearing round their necks medallions like Pong Ping's. "Why, of course, you're the Emperor's messengers!" he exclaims happily. Then, making signs that he will return soon, he runs to find Pong Ping.

Rupert doesn't have far to go, for Pong Ping has come out to see what all the noise and shaking is about. "Quick!" shouts Rupert, "your friends from the Emperor are here! They didn't come by airplane after all. They were in a sort of tank thing that goes under the ground!" At first Pong Ping can't understand what Rupert is talking about, but then he spots the strangers and rushes towards them, chattering excitedly. "Oh, I do wish I knew what they were saying," thinks Rupert.

RUPERT GETS A SURPRISE TRIP

A ride for Rupert is proposed.
They jump in and the door is closed.

The strange machine with mighty roar,
Descends into the earth once more.

At length they reach a distant land
With mountains very steep and grand.

"We'll leave you now," the two men say.
"You cross that bridge to find your way."

Pong Ping turns to Rupert. "You're quite right," he says. "They are from the Emperor and they've come to take me to him. But let's have a joyride first, shall we?" "Rather!" cries Rupert. So they scramble in and shut the door. But at once the machine plunges back into the hole from which it came. Rupert shouts at the driver to turn back but he doesn't understand. Then he turns to Pong Ping who is smiling mischievously. "I told him to do that," says the Peke. "I want you to come with me on holiday! Sorry, Rupert, but I do like to have someone with me and I'm sure you'll like it." "Oh, well—," Rupert agrees. But he still finds the journey through the earth long and dark and he is relieved when they emerge beside a river. After Pong Ping and the two men have spoken together, the little Peke says, "They say we must make our own way from here. They've told me what we must do. They say that first we have to make for that bridge over there. So let's go."

RUPERT SUMMONS THE BIRDS

They cross the bridge named by their guide,
And come upon a mountain side.

And there they see, as they were told,
A trumpet that is plainly old.

The trumpet's notes sound loud and clear.
And now two splendid birds appear.

"Come, scramble on our backs," they cry.
They stretch their wings and off they fly.

The bridge, when they come to it, is very steep and seems to lead nowhere but the steep sides of a high mountain. But Pong Ping doesn't hesitate. He leads the way upward until at last he stops and points to a crevice in the rock. Rupert can just make out a kind of trumpet. "That's what I was told to look for," says Pong Ping. "We have to blow it. Since you're stronger than I am you'd better do the blowing." Mystified, Rupert climbs up and takes the strange instrument.

He puts the trumpet to his lips and blows. To his delight it makes a loud, beautiful sound. Almost at once, in answer to the call, two great birds appear from beyond the mountain and fly towards the chums. "Climb on to our backs and hold tight!" they cry as they land. That is a lot easier said than done because their feathers are so smooth, but at length the pals are in position. "Off we go!" cry the birds, and with that launch themselves into space.

RUPERT MEETS THE EMPEROR

They cross a mighty mountain range
To reach a palace rich and strange.

An armoured soldier halts the pair,
And fixes them with frightening stare.

Pong Ping displays his medal rare.
The man at once admits the pair.

Then to the Emperor's room they're shown,
And find him seated on a throne.

High over the mountains fly the great birds with Rupert and Pong Ping clinging to their backs. At first Rupert can hardly bear to open his eyes but when he does so he sees a magnificent city below. Its buildings have spiky roofs and bright-coloured walls. "The Emperor's secret city," says the bird as it descends. The two birds put the pals down on a sort of terrace. Just as Rupert is wondering what happens next a fierce-looking soldier appears and says something Rupert doesn't understand.

Pong Ping, though, seems to understand for he produces his medallion and shows it to the soldier. The man studies the medallion and when he hands it back to Pong Ping he is much more respectful. Beckoning the pals to follow, he leads the way to a very large room where a friendly-looking man is seated on a throne. "The Emperor!" gasps Pong Ping. "Oh, and that must be his pet dragon." Just then the Emperor smiles and beckons to them to approach.

RUPERT IS GIVEN A WARNING

At supper Rupert's in a fix;
He finds he has to use chopsticks.

A hissing startles Rupert Bear.
He turns. A dragon's lurking there!

The dragon shouts, "It is a shame!
I've been neglected since you came!"

"My dreaded uncle flying there
Will carry off your friend, young bear."

"My old favourite's son! Welcome, welcome!" cries the Emperor. And Rupert is delighted to hear the kindly ruler speak a language that he understands. "Well, you must be hungry after your long journey," the Emperor goes on, and almost at once the friends find themselves at a table with a wonderful meal in front of them. Rupert, though, does have a bit of trouble with his chopsticks at first. Later when they set out to tour the palace, Rupert, who is lagging behind, hears a hiss from a corner and turns to find the Emperor's pet dragon. To his horror it grabs him by the scruff of the neck and drags him out on to a wide terrace. "Listen," it hisses. "I was the Emperor's favourite till your friend came. Tell him to go back at once or my uncle, the Flying Dragon, will put an end to him—understand?" He points towards the sky and there Rupert sees the sinister form of the great Flying Dragon.

81

RUPERT'S PAL IS CARRIED OFF

That night when both are fast asleep,
The dragon towards them starts to creep.

Rupert is wakened by a squeak.
The dragon's got his pal, the Peke.

Then to the Emperor Rupert goes
And tells of Pong Ping's dragon foes.

"To you a travel-bird I'll lend
To help you find your little friend."

To Rupert's astonishment Pong Ping is not at all worried by the dragon's threat. "I am the Emperor's favourite," he says. "No one would dare touch me." But Rupert is still uneasy as they settle down to sleep that night. After their long journey the chums are so tired and sleep so soundly that neither sees the frightening figure that glares through their window just as dawn is breaking. It is a cry of fear that wakens Rupert who opens his eyes to see his chum being hauled through the window by a great scaly claw. "The Flying Dragon!" he cries and, leaping from bed, dashes to the Emperor's chamber to tell him. But to his dismay the Emperor does nothing but moan, "Oh, dear, the Flying Dragon! No one can do anything about that, I fear!" "Oh, please let *me* try to rescue Pong Ping!" cries Rupert. "Oh, well, if you like," says the Emperor helplessly. "I shall send you on a travel-bird after them." And he has a bird summoned.

RUPERT MEETS THE WISE WOMAN

The bird says, "To a cave we'll go.
A wise old woman's there, I know."

"And to her words you must give heed.
Without her help you can't succeed."

The wise old woman hears his tale
And says, "Your courage must prevail."

"This drink will make the dragon sleep
For many hours in slumber deep."

As Rupert climbs aboard the bird the Emperor says, "The bird will take you close to the lair of the Flying Dragon. But, oh dear, it is a most dangerous task you have taken on. Good luck!" The bird heads deep into the mountains where at last it sets Rupert down on a high rock. "On your own you can never get Pong Ping back," it says. "But in that cave down there lives a wise old woman. Ask her advice. If she won't help you then you will never succeed. I shall wait here for you." Rupert scrambles down to the cave and just inside it comes upon the wise old woman. She nods as he pours out his story. "You are a person of great courage, otherwise you would not have got so far," she says. Then, handing Rupert a flask, she goes on, "This is a secret mixture. Somehow you must get the Flying Dragon to drink it. If he does he will sleep for half a day and only then you may be able to rescue your friend. But it will not be easy. Good luck!"

RUPERT TRIES A TRICK

The bird takes Rupert all the way,
And says, 'I'll call here every day."

The dragon's eating from a tree,
But no Pong Ping can Rupert see.

"He never drinks" a lizard cries.
"You'll have to catch him otherwise."

"Because the drinking plan's no use,
I'll paint the dragon's tree with juice."

Rupert scrambles back to the bird which carries him the rest of the way to the lair of the Flying Dragon, a deep valley. "You must go on alone," it says. "Each evening two of us birds will return here in case you rescue your friend. Good luck!" And off it flies. So Rupert makes his way into the valley until a munching noise stops him. He edges forward and, peeping from behind a rock, sees the dragon eating the top branches of a tree. "How can I get it to drink the sleeping mixture?" Rupert wonders aloud. "He doesn't drink anything for fear of putting out the fire he breathes," pipes up a little voice. Rupert turns to see a very small lizard. "None of us here likes the Flying Dragon," it goes on. "So I'll tell you that your only hope is to paint the leaves of one of his food trees with your mixture." It points out a good tree and Rupert sets to, using his scarf to paint all its leaves with the sleeping mixture.

RUPERT'S TRICK WORKS

"My trick's worked!" Rupert cries in glee.
"The dragon's eaten all the tree!"

He finds the dragon lying still.
Can he the rescue now fulfil?

Towards the giant beast he creeps
To make quite sure the dragon sleeps.

But when in vain he hunts about,
He says, "I'll have to risk a shout."

When he has painted all the leaves Rupert finds a safe spot and settles down for the night. It is daylight when he wakens and once more he steals down into the valley. To his delight he finds that the Flying Dragon must have returned during the night and eaten up all of the tree. "After gobbling down all that sleeping mixture it can't have got far," he thinks and sets out to explore. And, sure enough, he soon comes across the tail of the dragon. The rest of it is hidden behind a

rock. But is it asleep? Holding his breath, he peeps round the rock. Ah! The dragon is fast asleep and gently breathing fire. "Whew!" Rupert lets out a sigh. Now to find Pong Ping. Keeping as quiet as he can, Rupert hunts among the rocks, but no trace of his pal can he find. "I'll just have to shout for him and risk wakening the dragon," he decides. He climbs on to a rock a little way from the dragon and shouts, "Pong Ping! It's me—Rupert! Where are you?"

RUPERT RESCUES PONG PING

When Rupert turns, his foe still sleeps,
But round a boulder Pong Ping peeps.

He says, to still poor Pong Ping's fright,
"The birds will meet us here tonight."

"Well done, brave bear!" the Emperor cries.
"My golden medal is your prize."

But now a courtier cries with fear,
"Oh, sire, these two must not stay here."

A slight noise from where the dragon lies asleep makes Rupert start and swing round. To his great relief the beast is still slumbering, and peeping from behind a nearby rock is Pong Ping, still in his pyjamas. In hurried whispers Rupert explains about the sleeping mixture. "But we must hurry before the mixture stops working!" he declares, and taking Pong Ping by the hand, leads him up the steep side of the valley to where the birds have arranged to come each evening. As they reach the spot two travel-birds appear and very soon the pals are flying back to the Emperor's palace which they reach as dawn is breaking. The kindly old ruler is delighted at Pong Ping's rescue and orders that Rupert be awarded a golden medal for his bravery. But the rejoicing does not last long. No sooner is Pong Ping properly dressed again than an aged courtier appears. "Majesty," he quavers, "these two must not stay here. Come, I shall show you the reason why."

RUPERT AND PONG PING FLEE

The courtier points towards the sky,
And there they see the dragon fly.

The chums are hurried out of sight
For fear of that fierce dragon's spite.

The Emperor says, "I can't, you see,
Keep you two longer here with me."

So down the cellar chute they slide;
A steep and dark and bumpy ride.

The old courtier leads the way on to the terrace and points at the sky. "There!" he cries. "The Flying Dragon! Awake once more and I am quite sure looking for its escaped captive. If he finds Pong Ping here he will breathe fire upon us in his anger and burn us all up!" "Oh, dear! Gracious me!" gasps the Emperor who, though kind, is not at all brave. "We'd better get them away." And at once a guard is summoned and told to take the two chums out of sight. The burly guard picks up Rupert and Pong Ping and, followed by the Emperor, hurries them deep into the palace cellars. He sets them down on two mats at the edge of a hole in the floor. "Sorry about this," the Emperor says. "Come again when things are a bit quieter." "Thank you," Pong Ping replies. "I should love it if things really *were* a bit quieter." The Emperor nods. The guard gives the chums a push—and then suddenly they are sliding downwards through the earth in pitch darkness.

RUPERT REACHES THE PLAIN

When they are nearly in despair
They shoot into the open air.

And Rupert gives a happy shout,
"It was from here we started out!"

They clamber down towards the plain
And see their driver once again.

And then a bird towards them flies.
"It brings a message," Rupert cries.

Faster and faster the chums slide down the steep, dark slope. Then suddenly the slope is not so steep, there is daylight ahead and they swish into the open where a smooth rock checks their speed and prevents their being dashed on to the boulders below. Gazing around, Rupert exclaims, "I know where we are! This is where we started from before we called the birds." And so very carefully the two chums climb down over the boulders to the river. They cross the steep bridge again and start across the plain. "See! There's the tank thing that brought us here!" Rupert cries. Just then the driver of the tank spies the pals and runs to them. To Rupert's surprise he finds himself grabbed by the man who chatters sternly at them. "He says we should still be at the palace," explains Pong Ping. "He has had no orders about us." But at that moment Rupert spies one of the Emperor's travel-birds with something in its beak.

RUPERT IS SAFELY HOME

"The Emperor's orders," says the bird.
The driver reads the royal word.

Then in his arms the chums he takes
And for the tank he quickly makes.

Loud rumbling gives the Bears a fright,
And then the tank comes into sight.

"You see this hole?" says Rupert Bear.
"We've been to Pong Ping's land down there."

The great bird lands beside the driver who takes a scroll from its beak, unrolls it and reads. "That's the Emperor's orders about you," the bird explains. "I tried to get here first but you travelled so fast I was left behind." The driver finishes reading and without a word he lifts the chums and hurries to the tank. "I think we're going home," gasps Rupert. "I hope so!" Pong Ping says. "I shall never be homesick for this part of the world again."

Sometime later, back in Nutwood, Rupert's Mummy and Daddy, who are on their way to ask the police if anything has been seen of Rupert, suddenly hear a rumbling and find themselves face to face with a strange machine. In another moment Rupert and Pong Ping have jumped out, the machine has bored its way back into the earth and Mr. and Mrs. Bear are peering, amazed, down the hole that goes to the Far, Far East. "I'll tell you all about it over supper!" laughs Rupert.

personal property. Everything else that he had drawn for Rupert had been kept by the *Express*, who owned the copyright, and the material was locked away in steel cabinets ready for any future use. When the time came round for the Annual to be due for editing the precious stockpile would then be carefully gone through, and story sequences that had appeared in newspapers perhaps years earlier would be pulled out and printed up on acetate film for the colourist. Since 1954 the principal artist responsible for colouring the Annual has been Doris Campbell, and her skill has helped to create some of the best examples of children's book illustration in British publishing.

Origami, the art of paper-folding, has been a feature of postwar Annuals, and even formed part of stories, such as *Rupert and the Hobby-Horse*.

In 1949 Alfred Bestall exhibited at the Royal Academy summer exhibition a painting of the countryside near Oxted, Surrey, an area in which he liked to go for strenuous walks. He had long been fond of the open air and rock climbing, and was particularly drawn to the hills of North Wales, having remembered the area from his schooldays at Rydal. A frequent question he is asked is where the Nutwood countryside is supposed to be. Its dense woods and soft, distant hills evoke various places. He claims that it is an amalgam of the scenery in the Weald, the wooded plateau so loved by the poet Hilaire Belloc that lies in Kent and Sussex between the North and South Downs, and also of the Severn Valley around Hereford, with the more rugged terrain required in the stories reminiscent of the mountains of Snowdonia. They are all areas which he knows well, and covered in his rambles.

In early postwar years, as paper rationing eased and it became possible for other publishers to bring out rivals to the Rupert Annual it was felt that some new idea would be necessary to retain a high volume of sales. Alfred Bestall remembers as a child going to a Christmas party, which he says, with his characteristic clear-minded recall, was in 1899, and witnessing an amazing display of paper-folding, a skill known in Japan as origami. He was shown how to make a paper

boat and, having mastered the construction of it from a single sheet, spent the rest of the party wearing it as a hat. So he suggested to Stanley Marshall that he devise some easy figures that could be made. In the first postwar Annual the young readers were given the directions for making a bird out of a piece of paper. It was a sufficiently intriguing innovation to be tried in the following year, and soon a page of paper-folding instructions was a popular element in the Annual's contents. Readers from all over the world sent in their ideas, some of which would be used. There was even a kettle made from paper, which could actually be used to heat water.

A magician, called Robert Harbin, then well-known for his television programmes in which he often displayed his skill in the craft, formed the Origami Society, and invited Bestall to be its first honorary member. Later he became its President, and is in constant contact with a wide-ranging membership, which besides perpetuating the traditional designs also creates new ones. Virtually all the ancient patterns that are known have now been used in the Annuals, presenting problems for the future, but it is a popular feature and the better ideas are always welcomed at the *Daily Express*.

In 1948 Mary Tourtel died in the town of her birth, Canterbury, where she had returned for her final years. In its obituary

HOW TO MAKE A "HOBBY-HORSE"

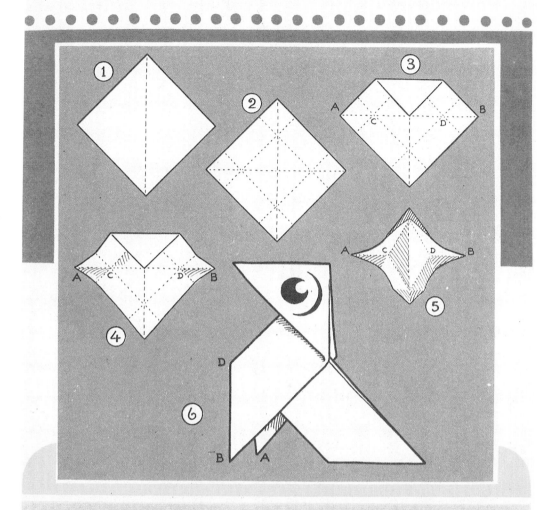

The Hobby-Horse that came to Rupert in the last story is one of the easiest of the paper-folding tricks and to make it you take a square of paper and fold it corner to corner to make the crease marked in Fig. 1. Turn the paper over and fold the other two corners together; then fold each side to the middle, so that the pattern of the creases is like Fig. 2. Next turn the paper over again, fold the top corner down to the middle line and leave it there (Fig. 3). Now pinch the corners A and B together and, holding them tight, push the spots marked C and D towards each other as in Figs. 4 and 5. When C and D are touching bring the points A and B together downward. Press all the folds firmly into place, draw an eye on each side of his head and your Hobby-Horse is finished.

report the *Express* noted how she had sent a message wishing the bear success every Christmas, and how she had congratulated the paper for achieving sales of 861,000 with the Rupert book that year, a world record for a children's annual. Later the figure would soar towards a million-and-a-half, but in the mid-Eighties it has settled back to around a quarter-of-a-million, which is still a figure that most publishers would contemplate with envy.

From the time of Mary Tourtel's death Alfred Bestall began to sign his Rupert drawings – hitherto he had not applied his signature, although she had always signed hers, and invariably also had her name incorporated in the typeset heading of the newspaper feature. It was a courtesy he had taken on himself to observe, although insiders were well aware of his existence, and the same report on Mary Tourtel's death acknowledged the manner in which he had carried on after her 1935 retirement. Occasionally he had playfully inserted his initials in a drawing, perhaps on a suitcase, as an in-joke for the amusement of more erudite readers. But from 1948 onwards the most sharp-eyed of them would notice discreetly tucked in a corner the word 'Bestall'.

After he had completed his first fifteen years as Rupert's artist, the timespan that Mary Tourtel had devoted to the bear, another tragedy occurred. 'Uncle Bill', Stanley Marshall, shortly after advising Bestall, prophetically as it happened, that he would be good for drawing Rupert for another fifteen years, himself died, and another era at the *Express* came to an end. He was succeeded as children's editor by Frederick Chaplain, who had for many years been involved in the production of comics for young children, including such famous titles as *Rainbow*, and *Mickey Mouse Weekly*, which was produced by Odhams in gravure. Chaplain, known in the office as 'Chappie', was a prolific source of ideas for stories, and could dash out the celebrated Rupert couplets with disarming ease. Eventually he was respon-

sible entirely for the Adventure stories, leaving the daily newspaper Rupert in the hands of Alfred Bestall.

Without his presence it is unlikely that Alfred could have gone on serving Rupert for so long. Chaplain helped him through the difficult early Fifties, and although many followers would disagree, his own assessment includes some of his best work in the later period. It is noticeable that there is a considerable difference in the style of his drawing. The precise, delicate line of early Bestall gives way to a much broader, more confident approach, and even Rupert looks different, with a longer snout and a rounder face.

With Alex Cubie and Enid Ash collaborating with Bestall, the Adventure series was able to continue until it had reached its fiftieth book in the summer of 1963. It was then decided to wind it up, after an attempt to convert it to an educational series in which the bear was used to teach the fundamentals of arithmetic, as well as support learning puzzles, failed to take off.

Alfred Bestall finally stopped drawing the daily Rupert in 1965. His last published story was 'Rupert and the Winkybickies', which ended on 22 July of that year. It was an appropriate time to call a halt. His mother had died in the previous year, having attained the magnificent age of 100, but the strain for him of breaking up the old home in Surbiton had been great. He also had to make arrange-

The selling of Rupert – merchandising licences have been granted to the manufacturers of toiletries, confectionery, crockery, mats, towels, bags, stationery, games, puzzles, toys and many other items.

ments for his handicapped, and now elderly sister, and bought a bungalow for her at Saltdean, near Brighton, where she could be looked after. She died in 1972. Alfred Bestall, who had never married, largely because he had, until the age of 45, when his speech impediment was cured, been desperately shy and withdrawn, had remained close to his mother, and now, even though he was over 70 himself, felt orphaned and alone. 'It was an anxious time because there were no relations to call upon. Almost all my relations of an active age are on the other side of the world, in Australia and New Zealand. There was virtually no-one in England.'

In spite of the accumulation of personal catastrophe he was to retain many of his links with Rupert. The Annual benefitted greatly from his services, and for many years was to carry only reprints of his stories. Only in the late Seventies was the work of succeeding artists admitted. He also painted the end-papers, producing some of his most enchanting work, such as 'The Frog's Chorus', so skilfully adapted into an animated cartoon film by Geoffrey Dunbar, accompanying Paul McCartney's music in the short film released in late 1984.

The covers of the Annuals, too, continued to be drawn by Bestall until 1973. In that year the tradition of the brown-faced Rupert on the cover was broken, allegedly following a query by Sir Max Aitken, the son of Lord Beaverbrook and at that time the owner of the *Express*. The amendment was made without consulting Bestall, who was particularly grieved since he had shown Rupert against a white sky, and the white face was artistically wrong, for it should have been in deep shadow. A few scarce examples of the brown-faced 1973 Annual exist, and are perhaps the rarest versions of a perennial book which is generally regarded as a good collectors' item. Bestall at this point decided to call it a day, and from then onwards the covers were painted by Alex Cubie, and the talented John Harrold, who is now, among those artists who have carried on with Rupert, regarded as the one who has come closest to the Bestall approach and imagination. His portrayal of the bear is brilliant, although Bestall, who has never met him, feels that he has yet to master some of the other characters, but greatly admires his work As far as the daily newspaper feature is concerned, Harrold is not responsible for the stories themselves,

1
さっきから　おにわで、も
ので　木をきるおとがしてい
ます。こぐまのルーバーは、
「あっ　だれか木をきっているん
だな。」と、いって　にわへ　か
けていきました。それは　おとう
さんぐまが、にわ木の下枝をおる
していらっしゃるのでした。

2
「おとうさん　ぼく、おてつ
だいしましょうか。」と、ル
ーバーがいうと、おとうさんは
にこにこしていいました。
「もう、おしまいだよ。それより
もぼうや、枝の中から、まっすぐ
なのをさがして　おかあさんに糸
をつけてもらって　つりに　あい
き。」

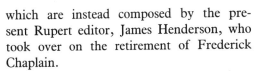

which are instead composed by the present Rupert editor, James Henderson, who took over on the retirement of Frederick Chaplain.

Henderson invited Bestall to continue making contributions to the Annual, such as decorative titles and the contents page, but with the passage of years inevitably the work has been harder for him to accomplish. He has a long-standing commission to produce a map of Nutwood, but has constantly put off the assignment because not surprisingly, over the 30 years in which he was actively involved in producing the Rupert stories, he was not always consistent in detailing the surrounding topography – for instance, the Wise Old Goat's castle might in one story take a day

and night to reach and in another be glimpsed above the trees only a short distance from the Bears' cottage. More importantly, he regards Nutwood as a state of mind, too diffuse to be pinned down within the formal limits of a map. John Harrold, with singular enthusiasm on the other hand, produced an end-paper for the 1984 Annual which quite clearly showed the geographic relationship of many landmarks in the stories, and as far as certain purists were concerned was guilty of putting them far too closely together, a charge that cannot be substantiated.

Henderson, too, incurred the wrath of the most dedicated Rupert devotees, by altering the page size of the Annual. The sound marketing argument was that with the adoption of standard EEC book formats the old page size was no longer appropriate, and if the Rupert Annual was to remain competitive it would have to switch to that now used by all the other children's annuals. Booksellers, particularly the large chains, dislike odd shapes, and are more likely to designate display space to a group of books all sharing the same format. Henderson has found that in spite of the validity of his case there is no way in which the traditionalists can be convinced. Although the primary market is young children, who are only likely to own a few Annuals during their childhood, it is the collectors (and there are several in Britain who have complete sets) find that the larger page size sits uneasily on their shelves, and accuse Henderson of change for change's sake. It is sometimes forgotten by the enthusiasts who have turned the collection and study of Rupert memorabilia into an absorbing hobby that as far as the *Daily Express* is concerned the principal reason for the continuation of the adventures into their seventh decade is that they are still capable of generating revenue and readers. Fleet Street is a commercial institution, and cannot for very long sustain features whose appeal is in decline. Before James Henderson changed the format the circulation of the Annual had been going down in the face of heavy alternative titles, often inspired by television series, but since the facelift that trend has been reversed, and the figures, while a long way short of the pre-TV heyday, continue to make satisfactory entries in the company's balance sheet.

What still remains sacrosanct in the Rupert Annual is the layout of the pages. Each of them still has four, almost square, drawings captioned with couplets, with a text narrative running across the foot, while at the top, beneath the story title in italics is a headline appropriate to that page alone, and flanked by small thumbnail drawings of Rupert and one of the other characters. Convention decrees that Rupert must always be on the outside. At one time Lord Beaverbrook had the idea that each figure should be drawn in a sequence so that when the edges of the pages were flicked the bear would appear to dance into life, but in spite of the simplicity of such a notion it has not actually been attempted.

Back in 1956 Alfred Bestall had taken a cottage in his beloved hills of North Wales, in the centre of the Snowdon National Park and superb climbing and walking country. There he spent many happy summers.

'I came to this district for a holiday the first time sixty-five years ago. I was advised by a clergyman that I would never find a better place to take my holidays. I became so smitten with it that I came every year after that – I don't think I ever missed one – and I became

more and more determined to have a place of my own.'

He used to spend six or seven fortnights a year in his remote and tranquil Welsh home, except in school holidays when his friends were accustomed to bringing their children. In September 1980 he decided to move away from Surbiton, where he had occupied a succession of flats, and live in his Welsh cottage permanently. When he returns south, which he does frequently, as he has many links with the south-western suburb, he stays with friends of long standing. 'I regard it as pretty essential to get down there three times a year. They are apt to ask me down there for my birthday, now that my birthdays are becoming rather impressive!'

His little single-storey cottage is in the Snowdonian village of Beddgelert, looking out across a broad valley and the fast-flowing River Glaslyn, and proud mountains beyond. It is one of the finest views in Britain, on his very doorstep, and a peaceful setting for him in his later years. At the rear of the house is a steep rocky outcrop, and his title extends almost to the top of the escarpment. 'I call this my back garden,' he says, pointing to a 200-foot almost sheer cliff face. Near the top are a number of unobtrusive whitewashed dots which denote his boundary line. Until relatively recently he would regularly make the strenuous climb to freshen them up.

At the time of writing he is 92 and, apart from minor infirmities, in reasonable health. At the age of 90 he broke his hip, playing table tennis (or ping-pong as he calls it) of all things, and was obliged to tone down his active regime. More recently he fractured his left arm, and was obliged to spend several weeks staying with Surbiton friends. But as soon as he was able he sped back to his cottage at Beddgelert. There he spends his time dealing meticulously with correspondence, much of which comes from Rupert followers of all ages, as well as greeting the occasional visitor, and drinking in the incomparable air. He still drives, and claims to be steadier behind the wheel than on his feet,

TEXT CONTINUES ON PAGE 111

RUPERT

"Ask Widow Goat to come to tea.
When you go to the shops for me."

It is Christmas Eve and Mrs. Bear is making a last check of her supplies to make sure she has all she needs. "Just a few small things to get from the shop," she says, "so perhaps you'll get them for me, Rupert." In fact, Rupert is glad of the chance of a trip into the village and sets off cheerfully armed with a shopping list. "By the way," Mrs. Bear says as he leaves, "drop in at Widow Goat's and invite her round to tea."

A complete Rupert adventure drawn by John Harrold.

and the Cuckoo Clock

Rupert sets out with his list.
ut doesn't see the rising mist.

The fog is now as thick that he
The Widow's house can hardly see.

So off Rupert goes, studying the shopping list as he heads for Widow Goat's cottage. What he does not notice is the thick fog creeping up behind him. By the time he is aware of it Widow Goat's cottage is in sight and he doesn't think it is worthwhile turning back. He approaches the cottage door and knocks. He waits. But nothing happens. He knocks again, but still no answer. Then from inside he hears a strange little sound.

He knocks. A little sound he knows
But no old Widow Goat appears.

RUPERT MEETS THE HOARSE BIRD

"Perhaps," he thinks, "I should explore."
And so he gently tries the door.

The sound comes from a cuckoo clock.
His nearness gives the bird a shock.

But Rupert coaxes it to speak
And learns the fog's made its throat weak.

"Some medicine you clearly need,"
Says Rupert and goes off at speed.

"I better have a look inside just in case there is something wrong," thinks Rupert. The silence broken only by that little noise worries him. He pushes open the door and steps inside. The place is empty. "Widow Goat?" he calls gently. Silence. Then suddenly the curious sound again. He spins round to where it comes from. And it seems to come from a cuckoo clock where the cuckoo is peering out of his little door. When it catches sight of Rupert it retreats, shutting the door.

Rupert climbs onto a chair so that his face is level with the clock's. "What's wrong?" he asks gently. "You don't sound well." The little door opens and the cuckoo looks out. "Oh, dear!" it croaks. "It's this English winter fog. It gets into my throat so. If I don't get some medicine soon I shall have to give up telling the time." "You poor thing!" Rupert exclaims. "I'm on my way to the shops. I'll try to get something for you." And off he goes into the thickening fog.

RUPERT GETS THE MEDICINE

He gets the shopping in a trice,
Then asks the chemist his advice.

The chemist says he feels quite sure
His stuff the cuckoo's throat will cure.

"The cuckoo clock of Widow Goat,"
He says, "has got a husky throat."

"Now," Rupert cries, "I must make haste!"
Says Mr. Bear, "Let's have a taste."

As soon as he has done his Mummy's shopping Rupert hurries round to Mr. Chimp the chemist. "Something for a cuckoo with a husky throat?" repeats Mr. Chimp when Rupert has explained what he wants. "H'm, let's see ... unusual, I must say, but I think I can let you have something that will do." And off he goes to make up a special mixture. When he hands it to Rupert he warns, "Be sure to let the cuckoo have only a drop at a time. It is very strong."

"What's that little bottle you have there?" asks Mrs. Bear when Rupert returns with her shopping. So Rupert explains how Widow Goat was not at home and how he found the cuckoo with the sore throat and got some special medicine for it from the chemist. Mr. Bear who has heard all this says, "Medicine for a cuckoo's sore throat? Whatever next. I must try this." "Well, only a sip," says Rupert as Mr. Bear fills a teaspoon with the medicine. "It is very strong."

RUPERT'S DADDY TRIES A DOSE

He sips. Now what's he going to do?
He's going to sing. He does—"Cuckoo!"

"Cuckoo! Cuckoo!" He doesn't stop
Until he makes a picture drop.

Although it's foggy Rupert goes
To give the clock cuckoo its dose.

It's lucky Rupert knows the way.
In fog so thick he might well stray.

Mr. Bear raises the teaspoon to his mouth, sips, swallows and smacks his lips. A strange look comes over his face after a moment. Rupert recognises it. It's the look he has when he is about to sing at one of the Nutwood village concerts. He shuts his eyes, takes a deep breath and opens his mouth. "Cuckoo!" he sings—or rather bellows. "Cuckoo! Cuckoo!" He makes such a tremendous noise that a picture is shaken off the wall and crashes to the floor. "My, it is strong!" Rupert gasps.

As soon as the effect of the medicine wears off and Mr. Bear can speak in his normal voice again, Rupert asks if he can take the medicine to Widow Goat's cuckoo clock. "It really did sound rather ill," he coaxes his Mummy who is not very keen about letting him go out in the fog. But when he convinces her that he knows the way too well to get lost she allows him to go. Yet, well as he knows the way, Rupert has to go very slowly from one landmark to the next.

RUPERT CURES THE CLOCK BIRD

They tell him that the Widow comes
By this time every day with crumbs.

Before he looks for Widow Goat
He treats the cuckoo's husky throat.

Now hear that clock bird cry "Cuckoo!
I feel so well now, thanks to you!"

The birds outside look and cry,
"Let us have some. Oh, do let's try!"

When at last Rupert reaches Widow Goat's home he finds several small rather anxious birds in the porch. "Where's Widow Goat?" they twitter. "Do you know? She's been away for ages. She ought to have been back by now to give us our crumbs." "Perhaps she's got lost in the fog," Rupert says. "Just let me give this medicine to the cuckoo in the clock and then I'll have a look for her." Then he goes inside, climbs onto the chair and gives the cuckoo his dose.

For a moment or two the cuckoo says nothing. Then quite suddenly it gives a loud, clear cry of "Cuckoo! Cuckoo! Cuckoo!" It pauses only long enough to say, "Oh, this is fine! I haven't felt so well for ages!" And off it goes again with its "Cuckoo!" Poor Rupert is wondering how on earth he can get it to stop when he hears a noise at the window and turns to see a crowd of birds. "Can we have some medicine?" they cry. "It seems to have done the cuckoo so much good!"

RUPERT PLAYS A TRICK

"That stuff is not for you, I fear,"
Says Rupert. Then a shape looms near!

It's Widow Goat who says she found
Her way home by the cuckoo's sound.

Says she, "Now you must stay for tea,
And you shall feed the birds for me."

Then Rupert, joking, thinks, "I'll spread
This medicine among the bread."

Rupert hurries out to explain to the birds that the medicine is only for cuckoos. From the porch he sees a shape loom through the fog. It looks quite eerie for a moment before he sees with a sigh of relief that it is Widow Goat. It turns out that she has been lost in the fog. "If I hadn't heard my cuckoo clock and made for the sound goodness knows where I might have ended up," she says. "But why does it sound so loud and clear?" So Rupert tells her what happened.

Widow Goat is so grateful for what Rupert has done for her cuckoo clock that she insists he stays for a meal. Afterwards she hands him a slice of bread and asks him to break it up for the birds who are still waiting for their crumbs. Rupert sees a chance to play a joke on the birds. When Widow Goat's back is turned he pours some of the cuckoo's throat medicine over the crumbs. "It can't do them any harm," he chuckles. "And won't Widow Goat get a surprise!"

RUPERT FINDS A BELL

"Crumbs!" Rupert calls and down they fly.
They eat. They pause. "Cuckoo!" they cry.

Gasps Widow Goat, "What have you done?"
But all the birds join in the fun.

The birds pretend they're cross and chase
The little bear. It's quite a race!

Then suddenly he gets a scare.
A bell falls through the foggy air!

The birds swarm round when Rupert takes the crumbs outside and scatters them. The birds eat them all up and for a moment there is a rather surprised sort of silence. Then "Cuckoo! Cuckoo! Cuckoo!" The noise from the birds is so loud that Widow Goat throws open her window to find out what on earth is going on. At that the birds join in the joke and crowd round her calling "Cuckoo!" until she has to close her window to shut out the din.

Rupert tells the birds that the effects of the medicine will soon wear off and they will sound like their old selves again. They pretend to be angry at this and in fun chase Rupert away from the cottage. After a little Rupert realises that the birds have turned back and that he has lost his way. While he is looking around, something falls very lightly on his head and bounces to the ground. It is a lovely, shiny little bell that weighs hardly anything at all.

RUPERT MEETS THE REINDEER

When Rupert lifts it from the ground
It tinkles with the sweetest sound.

He calls then scrambles up the tree,
But no one's there that he can see.

Horace Hedgehog has heard the bell.
But whose it is he cannot tell.

Then Rupert nearly drops with fright.
A reindeer leaps down into sight!

Rupert picks up the little bell. It tinkles sweetly as he lifts it. "Now where did that come from?" he wonders aloud. "Someone or something must have dropped it from this tree. Hello! Is there anyone up there?" There is no answer. "The tree's the only place I can see it could have come from," thinks Rupert. "I'll climb up and have a look." Being very good at climbing he is soon among the highest branches but there is no sign of anybody. When he reaches the ground again he sees an old friend Horace Hedgehog who has been attracted by the tinkling of the bell. But even Horace who knows most things that go on around the common has no idea whose bell it is. Suddenly there is a swishing noise from above and Horace who is very timid disappears into the fog. Rupert looks up and gets such a shock. For down through the fog bounds a reindeer. "That bell's mine," it says. "It fell off my harness. I heard you ringing it. Thank you so much."

RUPERT AGREES TO HELP SANTA.

The reindeer asks, "Please be so kind,
And fix my bell, if you don't mind."

"Now," says the reindeer, "back to work.
But ride with me above this murk."

Then high above the trees they fly
To where a sledge is standing by.

It's Santa Claus, by fog delayed.
"I'm lost," he says, "and need your aid."

"Be a good chap and fix the bell to my harness again," asks the reindeer. Still wondering what all this is about, Rupert obliges. "Thanks," the reindeer says. "Now for being so kind would you like to come with me and meet my master?" And so curious is Rupert that he can't resist the offer. He climbs onto the reindeer's back. "Where is your master?" he asks. "At the top of this tree?" "Not exactly," replies the reindeer. "You'll see." And he bounds into the air.

Up, up goes the reindeer with Rupert clinging to its harness. Up beyond the tops of the trees. Up until they break free of the fog into the evening sunshine above. "There's my master, over there," the reindeer calls. And on top of a cloud a little way off is another reindeer and a sledge, and on the sledge—rather as Rupert was beginning to expect—is Santa Claus. "Can you help me?" are Santa's first words. "I started my rounds early because of this fog. Now I'm lost."

RUPERT'S 'CUCKOOS' GUIDE HIM

Nutwood lies somewhere there below.
But where exactly they don't know.

Poor Santa can't believe his ears.
They can't be cuckoos that he hears!

"Not cuckoos!" Rupert cries in glee.
"Just plain birds who were tricked by me!"

They leave the clear bright sky behind,
And in the fog Nutwood they find.

Of course, Rupert is delighted to help Santa Claus and he scrambles aboard the sledge. "I'm looking for Nutwood," says the old gentleman. "Nutwood?" cries Rupert. "Why, that's where I live." But finding Nutwood is much harder than Rupert thought. The billowing fog beneath them gives no clue to what lies below it. Suddenly Santa cups his ear and cries. "What on earth is that noise down there? If I didn't know that this was England and that it is winter I'd say those were cuckoos." Rupert jumps up in delight. "No, they're not cuckoos and this is Nutwood right under us now," he cries. "Oh, please go down now!" And while Santa eases his sledge through the fog Rupert pours out the story of the cuckoo clock and the throat medicine. "Well, I never! Well, I never!" Santa keeps saying until Rupert breaks in with, "That chimney there. I recognise that. It's the one on my house. Hooray! Hooray! We've reached Nutwood, Santa!"

RUPERT LABELS THE PRESENTS

Says Santa, "I've been so delayed,
I can't stop here long, I'm afraid."

"Here's Bill!" cries Rupert. "And I know
To fetch our chums he'll gladly go."

So Santa empties out his toys,
And Rupert chooses for the boys.

The chums come running up just when
Santa is on his way again.

Guided by Rupert, Santa cruises his sledge over Nutwood having all the houses pointed out to him. At last he says, "Wait. I've an idea. This fog has held me up so much and I've so many other places to visit that I haven't time to go down all the chimneys in Nutwood. Show me where your common is and we'll land there and I shall hand out all the presents there." So down they go and the first person they see is a very startled Bill Badger. "Bill, hurry and fetch all our friends,"

Rupert pleads. Off Bill darts and while he is gone Rupert helps Santa sort out the toys for he knows exactly what each of his friends wants. With Santa ticking off the various presents on his list, Rupert writes out the labels for them, remembering when he writes "Happy Christmas" to sign it "Santa" and not "Rupert". By the time Bill returns with the others the presents are all ready and Santa is leaving. "You've been a real help, Rupert!" he calls back.

RUPERT GETS HIS REWARD

The happy chums agree that they
Will keep their gifts till Christmas Day.

Bill who's been counting, gives a shout,
"You've gone and left your own self out!"

He goes home feeling rather blue
Till Daddy says, "This came for you!"

And best of all—he might have known—
A cuckoo clock! His very own!

Rupert hands out the presents to his assembled pals and makes them promise that since they have had to be delivered early they won't start to play with them until next day. They all promise and it is only when most of them have scampered off home that Bill notices something. "Rupert," he asks, "where's your own present?" "Mine?" Rupert gasps. "My goodness! I forgot to put myself on the present list. Oh, I say, what an awful forgetful ninny I am!"

Although he acts cheerful Rupert really feels terribly disappointed as he walks home with his close pals. But just inside his front door his Daddy is standing, clutching a very big parcel. "Santa called a few minutes ago," he says. "He told me how you'd helped so much you forgot a present for yourself. He left this for you." Excitedly Rupert unwraps it. "Oh, wonderful!" he cries. "Something to remind me of this adventure —a cuckoo clock all of my own!"

but limits his forays to a mere 50 miles in one day, which is more than sufficient to get him to and from Porthmadog, his nearest town.

When inevitably reference is made to his astonishing longevity he points out that his is a long-lived family, and that his mother lived to be 100.

No visitor to his cottage is allowed to escape without being photographed, and he has filled several albums with colour prints of guests, among whom are Paul and Linda McCartney and their children, Terence Stamp the actor and Terry Jones, film-maker, member of Monty Python and children's storyteller, all of them dedicated Rupert followers. In 1982 Terry Jones made a documentary film on Rupert and Alfred Bestall, which was shown on Channel 4. As a consequence he found that people now recognised him when he was in public, and complete strangers would sometimes request his autograph and express their gratitude for the part Rupert had played in their formative years.

As another example of the new respect accorded him, Tony Shuker, a school-master in Newark, Nottinghamshire, formed an association called The Followers of Rupert which publishes a magazine for its members and other interested parties, *Nutwood*. In September 1984 Alfred Bestall made the long drive from North Wales to Newark and addressed the Followers who had gathered at a hostelry called the Robin Hood Hotel, and a transcript of the evening's proceedings was later published as a *Nutwood* Special. It is a constant source of surprise to him that anyone should take Rupert that seriously, and although he never got into the position in which Mary Tourtel found herself, of wanting to be rid of the character, he is often amused by some of the more high-flown commentaries on his work. *Nutwood* often discusses minutiae in great detail – differences in printing processes, variations in the portrayal of characters, interpretations of stories, the correct number of horizontal stripes on Rupert's trousers – so much so that

its pages sometimes a scholarly air more in keeping with the journal of a learned society. Bestall attempts to point out that he sometimes made mistakes, hence geographical variations, and that while he was always careful to maintain continuity within a single story, he did not always match details from one adventure to another, so that the Professor's castle might well pop up in another part of the forest, or a character's name might change completely. One example that was forced on him was Willie Mouse, who was originally called Willie Whiskers until it was politely pointed out that another publication already had a character of that name.

Another example of prodigious research and energy expended on Rupert scholarship is *The Rupert Index*, a private publication distributed by Norman Shaw of Upper Norwood, a leading dealer in children's publications from the 19th century to the present, and compiled by W. O. G. Lofts and Derek J. Adley. They have put together a bibliography of virtually every Rupert story ever published, with dates and other relevant information. To achieve it took months of patient delving through the fragile British Library newspaper files at Colindale, as well as combing book catalogues and hundreds of other references. The quantity of Rupert material is astounding, and since the publication of *The Rupert Index* more has come to light, including previously unacknowledged stories by Mary Tourtel, and the pages of *Nutwood*, which is unconnected, although the Messrs Lofts and Adley are prominent among the Followers, frequently carry updates and amendments to their intriguing work.

These stills are from Paul McCartney's award-winning short cartoon, *Rupert and the Frog Song*, released in late 1984, made with Geoffrey Dunbar as director of animation and based on Bestall's celebrated Frog's Chorus endpaper, previous pages.

Although it was not the intention, the interest in Rupert has sent the prices of old Rupert Annuals soaring, and some astute people have even seen them as profitable investments, and an alternative to stocks and shares. The Followers are not entranced by the intrusion of speculators into the field, as it has sent the prices of some material out of reach. Their own approach to collecting is based on the ancient principle of swapping amongst themselves, so that at Followers' meetings, although tables are often piled high with various items on the market, and trading appears to be brisk, very little cash actually changes hands.

Probably the finest collection of Rupert material is in the possession of Alan and Laurel Clark, a married couple whose commodious Victorian family house in a quiet Tunbridge Wells cul-de-sac has a whole room full of valuable items, which even the *Daily Express* itself has occasionally borrowed as their own archives have failed to yield some item, such as the dust-jacket of the first Annual, removed by some tidy-minded individual who filed the book without it. The Clarks should really be regarded not as obsessive collectors, but as serious social historians through whose efforts a corner of the history of British journalism and graphic design has been preserved.

They also possess a massive collection of Rupert merchandising, ranging from jigsaw puzzles produced in the Thirties to chocolate biscuits and paper handkerchiefs in the Seventies. In comparison with such long-lived American cartoons as Peanuts it might be felt that the *Express* was slow in capitalising on the commercial possibilities to be gained from the Rupert name. Syndication in other countries has been rare, although the Dutch have been devoted readers since Mary Tourtel's day. An adventurous Japanese publisher used some of the adventures, redrawing

them to fit a more aggressive style. But that was as nothing in comparison with the use made of Rupert in the pages of *Oz*, a journal of British counter-culture in the early Seventies, which published a legendary 'Schoolkid's Issue' that put its editors in dock at the Old Bailey.

In 1970 ITV began transmitting an animated puppet version of Rupert for afternoon children's viewing, and the series eventually reached more than 150 segments in the next seven years. By agreement with Century 21, the merchandising arm of the now former television contractor, ATV, a range of Rupert toiletries appeared, as well as a candy bar manufactured by Nestlé. There has always been caution in the allocation of licences for such products, as understandably the newspaper has not wanted the bear to be associated with anything that might be considered harmful for children.

There have also been stage productions featuring actors in animal costumes portraying Rupert and his friends, but the spin-off that should provide the most satisfying alternative to the Rupert of the printed page is the projected full-length animated film to be produced by Paul McCartney, with Geoffrey Dunbar as the director of animation. A 'taster' of the expected quality was released at the end of 1984 in the form of a short, *Rupert and the Frog Song*, based on one of Bestall's most celebrated endpapers, which won a British Academy of Film and Television Arts award, as well as another place in the charts for McCartney, who composed and performed the accompanying song. The development of the film is, however, likely to take several years, and may well not be ready for the public until the end of the Eighties, perhaps in time for Rupert's 70th birthday.

Meanwhile, Rupert appears not only every day in the *Daily Express*, but also each Sunday in full colour in the *Sunday Express Magazine*, and in 1985 not only does he celebrate 65 years of life as a newspaper feature, but the Annual reaches its fiftieth edition.

RUPERT IN QUEER STREET

It is Christmas Eve. Rupert and Podgy and Dinkie, the cat, have gone into a town to buy presents. "I say", cries Rupert, "just look where we are! I've heard my Daddy speak of Queer Street but I didn't really know there was such a place." A kindly policeman smiles at him. "If you look around you'll see why it's called Queer Street," he says.

There are more than half a dozen things wrong with the picture and they make it a very queer street indeed. Can you see what they are?

4

Long Live Rupert!

Although the original creation was that of Mary Tourtel, it was Alfred Bestall who lifted Rupert into the realms of great children's literature. Terry Jones, himself the author of children's fairy stories, is prepared to place certain of Bestall's Rupert Annuals alongside Lewis Carroll and Edward Lear, and he is not alone in regarding the adventures as immeasurably superior to those of A. A. Milne's Winnie the Pooh, part of the celebrity of which depended on the fine line illustrations of Bestall's contemporary, E. W. Shepard. Jones regards it as unjust that whereas Milne achieved fame and wealth Bestall is by comparison little known and lives modestly.

He began his Channel 4 film ingeniously, with a series of 'vox pop' street interviews, asking assorted people if they had ever heard of Alfred Bestall. Not a single person was able to answer that he had. He then asked the same people if they knew Rupert, and every one of them immediately affirmed that he was familiar with the little bear, and intrigued to learn of its connection with Alfred Bestall. Shortly after its second transmission on S4C, the Welsh version of Channel 4, my wife, son and I were having tea with Alfred Bestall in a teashop in Beaumaris, Anglesey, when the middle-aged woman at the cash desk recog-

nised him, and with characteristic Welsh courtesy thanked him for the pleasure he had given her and her children and requested his autograph. Such public recognition has taken him a long time to achieve, but it is largely due to the early anonymity and later very modest acknowledgement of his work.

What were the major differences between the Tourtel and Bestall approach to Rupert? Whereas Mary Tourtel's imagination, in spite of her graphic skill, was dependent on literary tradition, Alfred Bestall had developed his much more visually. In the Twenties he had been an avid filmgoer, and had been interested in the structure of the film itself, the way it was cut, so that viewpoints could be changed, settings suddenly switched, close-ups alternated with long shots. He loved the silent cinema largely because of the power of the image, and watched it reach its apotheosis during its last decade. When talkies arrived he was immediately aware of the sudden diminishing of visual quality, largely due to the necessity for a static camera during the early, primitive days of sound recording, as well as the dominance of dialogue over the picture, and he lost his former interest.

But films had taught him the value of developing a story by keeping the visuals

fresh. Mary Tourtel often retained the same background for frame after frame, merely altering the positions of foreground characters. Consequently there was a certain monotony in the way she let the story unfold. Bestall went out of his way to create contrast and excitement. He would constantly shift the point of view, and make every part of the almost square-shaped frame work. A square is not an easy area for an artist to compose within, but Bestall achieved it with apparent effortlessness, which was part of the illusion he created.

He also developed his stories with a great deal more ingenuity than Tourtel. She was averse to taxing the child's imagination where unravelling a plot was concerned. Bestall constructed his plots like a mosaic, letting the pieces seemingly fly at random until they were all drawn together for a solution. It would not be difficult to imagine him as a writer of mystery thrillers in another context, since there was often the feeling of a detective story, an ingredient which sustained the day-to-day interest, keeping young readers agog to find out what would happen next. The lengths of his stories varied, there being no set number of frames, but even when they were allowed to run on the interest of the reader was maintained by the careful thought that went into the weaving of an intricate narrative in which mysteries would eventually be satisfactorily resolved.

The 'long-shot' and the 'close-up' – an almost cinematic method used by Bestall to sustain the interest of his readers in a developing storyline. Opposite: more Bestall endpapers.

He also made Rupert a much more active and adaptable creation. His range of facial expressions was considerably enhanced, and his movements became freer, more boylike. Bestall avoided showing him in too much detail without his shoes, but since he has human hands it can be assumed that so too were his feet. The Wise Old Goat began with hooves instead of hands but Bestall arranged a transplant. When Rupert takes a bath the faintest impression of a fuzzy back is displayed. He is a boy with a bear's head. Only Edward Trunk is cursed with his elephant's feet, which make him a difficult character to work into a plot, as he cannot easily pick up objects.

Many of the Mary Tourtel characters were kept by Bestall, especially Rupert's inner circle of friends: Bill Badger, Edward Trunk, Algy Pug, Podgy Pig, Willie Mouse, the Rabbit twins, the Fox brothers, and of course Rupert's parents, Mr and Mrs Bear, he of the casual tweeds, later formalised into an elegant set of plus-fours, and she of the long chintz dresses and gingham aprons. But within a very short time of taking over he was bringing in a new cast of his own. The stricture against gratuitous magic in the stories was ingeniously circumvented by the introduction

TEXT CONTINUES ON PAGE 131

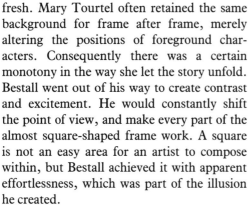

A gallery of some of Rupert's friends. Most of them date from Mary Tourtel's time. Podgy Pig is a food lover, a warm-hearted glutton. Edward Trunk is a gentle giant, a strong, amiable ally. Bill Badger is Rupert's oldest friend, cool in a crisis, always cheerful. Algy Pug, another very old pal, occasionally plays practical jokes. The Fox Twins, Freddy and Ferdy are, like the Rabbit twins, not members of the intimate circle, but frequently get themselves into scrapes from which they have to be rescued. Pong-Ping, a superb Bestall creation, is a rich Chinese friend, whose short temper is matched by his generosity. He also possesses a small dragon as a pet. Right: a charming Bestall drawing of the chums mounted on an old horse.

More Nutwood characters. Gregory Guinea Pig is often in trouble. Willie Mouse is a timid soul, but tries hard. Rosalie is Podgy's awful cousin, selfish and spoiled. Grandma Goat and Billy Goat are Nutwood neighbours. Bingo is a brainy pup, a high-IQ scholar who likes to know how things work.

Constable Growler, Dr Lion and Mr Chimp the schoolmaster are the professionals who keep the wheels of Nutwood turning, much as they always have done. The 20th century still seems to be young there, and Mr Anteater continues to go about his business in the garb of an interwar city gentleman.

The Professor is an amiable friend of Rupert who lives in a castellated tower on the edge of Nutwood and is constantly inventing extraordinary devices, often using advanced technology. His servant is an amusing little dwarf. The Wise Old Goat lives in a castle and is very mysterious indeed, having occult powers. The Chinese Conjuror is well-versed in oriental magic, and lives in a pagoda.

Rupert's human friends include Mary, who is quite contrary as far as her garden is concerned, the Boy Scout (still garbed as B-P himself would have liked), Peter, Margot, Tigerlily, the Chinese Conjuror's naughty daughter, and the three Girl Guides.

Gaffer Jarge, sometimes mistaken for Old Willum, appears to be Nutwood's oldest inhabitant, while Sailor Sam and Cap'n Barnacle are nautical personages more likely to be encountered at Sandy Bay, and the Merboy has been described by Alfred Bestall as 'a most useful character'.

Golly rarely appears now, while the Imps of
Spring and Simple Simon are similarly retiring;
Mr and Mrs Bear, and Uncle Bruno on the left,
are Rupert's immediate family, but he has a
strange, very bear like, Uncle Grizzly, who lives
in a cave in Arizona.

With hisses grim the snakes move fast,
While negroes, loudly shouting, fly.

The white men, too, in horror gasp,
Till they hear Rupert's valiant cry.

Such lapses in racial awareness as shown here would now get short shrift but in a former time were regarded innocently. The editor in charge of Rupert at the *Daily Express*, James Henderson, must scrutinise old drawings carefully before consenting to their re-use.

of a Chinese conjurer of fabled skill, and his impish daughter, Tigerlily, who could occasionally indulge in mischievous pranks with her father's wands.

Bestall also wanted a character who would be much brainier than the others, so he devised a bespectacled pup called Bingo who was the Nutwood school swot, and an amateur inventor, a canine polymath who, nevertheless, fitted happily into the circle of chums. Then there was Pong-Ping, another oriental emigré, a Pekinese of great wealth, and the proud owner of a pet dragon. It is a mistake to assume that the chinoiserie present in the Bestall Rupert was a harking-back to his own early childhood in the Far East. Rather more mundanely, perhaps, it was actually derived from his fondness for a celebrated long-running West End musical of the First World War and after, *Chu-Chin-Chow*, which provoked a craze for things Chinese.

He also created a number of human characters. There was the Professor, for example, a slightly bumbling, bald-headed inventor who lived in a distinctive, castellated tower that would protrude above the dense trees around Nutwood. He lived there with his servant, a small, black-garbed figure for some reason clad in a medieval costume with hose and pointed shoes. The professor enabled Rupert to come face-to-face with science and technology, amazing flying machines, wonderful radio apparatus, even computers. James Henderson claims that Bestall used an aircraft rocket-launch ramp long before the Royal Navy installed such devices on its carriers, in 'Rupert and the Rocket Plane' in the 1946 Annual.

Then there was Rollo, a gypsy boy, in tune with strange folklore that only travellers such as he and his old grandmother could know about. There is Mary, a figure straight out of the 'How does your garden grow?' nursery rhyme, who lives with her grandfather in a large house, and like him affects eighteenth-century dress. Another anachronistically attired human is Sailor Sam, a nineteenth-

century tar whose uniform and pigtails pre-date H.M.S. Pinafore. And also in the nautical idiom is the Merboy, a half-human who crops up now and again – 'a most useful character' according to Bestall.

It will be seen that all these people can open doors to marvellous adventures, and that is one of the elements that has given Rupert such staying power. For Rupert often has only to run into one of these characters, in the woods near his home, to be propelled into enchantment and adventure.

There is, of course, a resident band of Nutwood performers, the functionaries of the little community, such as Dr Lion and Constable Growler. The village school is run by an aged chimpanzee, Dr Chimp.

There are also, apart from the obvious villains, a few distinctly irritating characters, such as Rosalie, a cousin of the unfortunate Podgy, whose airs suggest that she is the prototype for Jim Henson's Miss Piggy.

During the latter days of Mary Tourtel there were occasional complaints from parents that her ogres and witches were too frightening and nightmarish for children, and Bestall was at pains to play this aspect down. Although Rupert's adventures were fantastic, and often would leave him in a difficult situation to be resolved on the morrow, care was taken to spare real horrors. In the recycling of stories for the Annuals it is occasionally necessary for minor details to be altered with discretion. Cigarette-smoking humans

TEXT CONTINUES ON PAGE 141

RUPERT'S FAIRY CYCLE

When Rupert meets his chums one day,
They think it's much too cold to play.

They settle down with pen and ink,
And of their Christmas presents think.

They post their letters in a tree,
And hope that Santa Claus will see.

When Pong Ping hears what they have done,
He laughs at them, and thinks it's fun.

Before it's really light next day
The little bear looks out that way.

When he has dressed, he runs to see
And meets friend Podgy near the tree.

Inside the tree peers Rupert Bear
And finds a different letter there.

From Santa Claus this one has come,
And Rupert reads it with his chum.

Rupert's Fairy Cycle

"Hullo!" cries Pong Ping, "how are you?
Here is a friend of mine—Li-poo."

"Please read this note," then Rupert cries,
"My chums are very sad," he sighs.

Then Li-poo says, "Just come with me;
About your present we shall see."

"I'm off to China now," he cries,
And Rupert watches in surprise.

A few days later Rupert's chum
Informs him that his cycle's come.

When Rupert looks he says, "Oh dear!
It certainly is so very queer."

He tries it in the lane outside,
But finds it very hard to ride.

Then suddenly the wheels whizz round:
They barely seem to touch the ground.

Rupert's Fairy Cycle

Outside his house he has a fall;
The cycle leans against the wall.

A small bird stops the little bear,
And warns him that he must take care.

Then next a squirrel Rupert sees,
who with the little bird agrees.

The squirrel climbs the tree in fright,
And very soon he's out of sight.

"I wish I could do that," he sighs,
And then the cycle starts to rise.

It stops so very suddenly,
But Rupert grabs hold of the tree.

The bird flies up to him again,
And chirps, "to you I must explain

"Whatever you would like to do:
That cycle makes your wish come true."

Rupert's Fairy Cycle

He wishes he was on the ground,
And there he is—quite safe and sound.

Thinks Rupert, shelt'ring from the storm,
"I'd like to be where it is warm."

He realises what he has done,
But finds his journey has begun.

The cycle glides high in the air,
Oh! What a thrill for Rupert Bear.

The cloud banks end and at great pace
Poor Rupert shoots off into space.

Then Rupert sees with great delight,
Two wings appear to help his flight.

Across the sea he flies so fast
And on an island lands at last.

Now Rupert soon goes fast to sleep,
And near him strange black figures creep.

Rupert's Fairy Cycle

A black man grabs him by the arm,
Which fills poor Rupert with alarm.

About his waist a rope they tie,
Then hoist him to a ledge on high.

When Rupert crawls on to the edge,
He sees the men beneath his ledge.

And then the black men down below
A coil of rope to Rupert throw.

They stand and watch the little bear,
As he descends the rope with care.

The savages want him to show
How they can make the cycle go.

The black men get a nasty shock,
To see the cycle climb the rock.

"My goodness!" gasps the little bear,
"I'm glad to get away from there."

136

Rupert's Fairy Cycle

But when he leaves the sky once more,
He finds he's worse off than before.

He sees a puffin sitting there,
Who says, "you're not a polar bear."

Poor Rupert cannot walk at all;
Each time he tries he has a fall.

A seagull up to Rupert flies,
"Be off before you freeze," it cries.

He says when safely on his seat,
"That Mandarin I wish to meet."

O'er woods and mountains Rupert flies,
And funny creatures fill the skies.

Once more he's filled with great alarm,
But finds they do not wish him harm.

Beside a tower he lands at last,
And finds the doors are shut quite fast.

137

Rupert's Fairy Cycle

Another fright for Rupert Bear;
He finds a dragon standing there!

When suddenly they open wide,
The Fairy cycle goes inside.

He's taken then to see Li-poo,
Who says "I was expecting you",

"I made that cycle," he explains,
"To use when any child complains."

Then Rupert says, "you're very good;
I think that I have understood."

"Alright," says Li-poo, "come with me,
This lovely temple you must see."

He proudly shows the little bear,
That there's a magic lift in there.

"What's wrong?" thinks Rupert with a frown;
He's slowly turning upside down.

Rupert's Fairy Cycle

When Rupert runs out of the door
In Nutwood he is safe once more.

While walking home he meets his chum;
Poor Podgy is looking very glum,

And Edward, too, is rather sad,
He burst the football that he had.

Then Rupert tells where he has been,
And all the wonders that he's seen.

Rupert has an affinity with the avian world, with the stately King Toucan its amiable ruler.

are no longer persona grata. James Henderson recalls one story in which Rupert visited a long-lost relation in America who turned out to be a grizzly, with bleached bones littering the floor of his cave, suggesting predatory attacks on unfortunate mountain climbers. Another problem that often arises is the changed modern attitude to matters of race. In the pre-war days no visit to the English seaside was complete without attendance at a beach concert given by a troupe of 'nigger minstrels', who were either white men in blackface makeup, or genuine black musicians. But such a term used nowadays would be likely to provoke serious offence, if not actually contravening the race relations legislation. Likewise, to designate a tropical landfall, full of grass-skirted, spike-haired natives, as 'Coon Island' may well have been innocent enough in 1946, but is unacceptable today.

Such lapses are few. The stories hold up surprisingly well, largely because they are timeless in tone. Topical references are almost non-existent, and Nutwood survives as it always has, ignoring the increasingly jaded twentieth century. Occasional forays into a big town take place, and Rupert has been known to ride on a bus, travel on a train and even go to the pictures, but the antique appearance of such things seems part of the Rupert tradition, and rarely bothers children. However, it has been necessary to update the uniforms of the three Girl Guides, who at the time of their debut in 1938 were clad in the belted Edwardian-style tunics and wide-brimmed hats decreed by Lady Baden-Powell when the movement was founded and which were still worn in the Thirties. Later, in 1946, the guides were drawn from life and began to feature regularly in Rupert's adventures. Beryl, Pauline and Janet were members of the 10th Surbiton guides and Bestall has kept in contact with the three girls over the years.

But the mixing of styles and costumes is as much part of the Bestall scene as it was with Tourtel. Just as the fact that Nutwood is populated by a mixture of humans and talking animals, all apparently co-existing in harmony, the manifestation of costumes and objects from another time period is never regarded as remarkable. If a seaside holiday at Sandy Bay, with its Devonian golden sands and pier entertainers is interrupted by the appearance of a pirate galleon in full sail, crewed by a gang of eighteenth-century cut-throats, the surreal quality of Bestall's Rupert is such that no-one finds the presence extraordinary, just a nuisance that has to be dealt with. Dragons, sea serpents and the more fanciful denizens of the strange kingdom of the birds, ruled over by a corpulent Toucan King, a Mary Tourtel character made much more endearing by Bestall, are among the many fanciful creatures who impinge upon the scene.

Also taken for granted are the curious forms of locomotion and travel available to Rupert and his friends. Readers of Rupert are as familiar with the 'time warp', a window through which one may pass to another era or another place as effortlessly as crossing a threshold, as are the devotees of the literature of science fiction. Pong-Ping has a secret means of getting directly from his house to China, a route Rupert has taken on more than one occasion. Ice floes, rafts of seaweed,

TEXT CONTINUES ON PAGE 156

Rupert often becomes airborne by a
variety of means, including the tiny
helicopter whose design was inspired
by a young reader. On occasion he
has even risen into the air without
visible assistance.

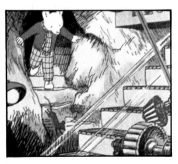

One of the most delightful of Bestall inventions was an underground railway specially for animals, which transported Rupert back from London, where he had been watching the Coronation, to Nutwood. There were no trains, locomotion being provided in the form of a rapidly-undulating floor which acted as a conveyor belt. Exit from the underground was by man-hole cover – solving, for Rupert, the ancient mystery of their purpose.

RUPERT
AND THE
MYSTERY POND

Here's Rupert asking leave to play
With Bill, and Mother says he may.

He starts at once, and just beyond,
A stranger gazes in a pond.

Now when the little Bear's nearby,
The stranger curtly calls out "Hi!"

"I'd like you, please, to rack your brain,
And this mysterious stream explain."

As Rupert hears this odd request,
The stranger measures round his chest,

And while the tape the man rewinds
A curious stick Rupert finds.

Just as he's pondering what to say
The stick is roughly snatched away.

And while he wonders what is wrong
The man goes angrily along.

148

Rupert and the Mystery Pond

Then, suddenly upon a hill
There stands young Rupert's old friend, Bill.

With arms outstretched they start to run,
And Bill asks Rupert what he's done.

Along a little lane they walk,
While fast and eagerly they talk.

Quite soon, to their surprise they see some
Pram wheels, "Look!" they shout with glee.

Then home the little wheels they take,
And there a trolley strong they make.

And Mrs Bear comes out to see
Just how they mean to have a spree.

They shove the trolley down the slope,
But with it now they cannot cope.

The wheels are fixed, and soon the pair,
Are flung off madly in the air.

Rupert and the Mystery Pond

Down in some undergrowth they fall,
But out of it, unhurt, they crawl.

And as around the rocks they peer,
Bill cries, "Do hush! a voice I hear."

"Help help!" They hear some feeble cries,
And then they see a hand arise.

It is the stranger they have found;
He's hurt and can't get off the ground.

They bring their trolley round the hill,
Then Rupert lifts, and so does Bill.

To Rupert Mr Bear attends,
And for a Doctor quickly sends;

While Rupert makes a bold request—
To solve the mystery for his guest.

And up the stony, rough-hewn road
They safety pull their heavy load.

Rupert and the Mystery Pond

"Then take this stick," the old man cries:
"It gives the clue if you are wise."

They study words, and carving, too,
To make the stick reveal the clue.

They write the words, then have a chat;
"'The Lake of Nutwood': where is that?"

Says Bill, "let's have another ride;
Perhaps we'll get ideas outside."

Cries Rupert, "I.S.—south, one mile;
Let's give that clue a little trial."

So, finding south by weathervane
They take their trolley out again.

They tramp along, and reach a wood,
And think this way can't be much good,

When Bill espies a curious light,
Set in a tree, and shining bright.

151

Rupert and the Mystery Pond

They rush, excited, to the tree
To find out what the light can be.

Bill climbs up first; shouts "Rupert, quick!
We're on the trail; do bring that stick."

Then Rupert, climbing, sees the bell
That's carved upon the stick as well.

He strikes the bell, out pops an owl
"Hullo! Who's there?" they hear him growl.

He sees the stick and says, "Now you
Must keep on south, a stone's the clue."

And so the pair move on in haste,
They haven't any time to waste.

Their trolley they have left behind;
They simply want the stone to find.

At length they think they've reached their goal
A stone that has a tiny hole.

Rupert and the Mystery Pond

Now in this hole the stick they fit,
Then on the stone, perplexed, they sit.

Soon Bill gets up and walks about,
And all at once he gives a shout.

For now their stick's long shadow lies
Upon a stone of smaller size.

They lift it to investigate
And find a handled, iron plate.

And there's a ladder leads below,
Down which brave Rupert says he'll go.

"The hole's so small," he shouts, "I've guessed
Why that old man sized up my chest."

Once down below he sees strange sights—
Caves, waterfalls, and greenish lights;

But when he turns his friend to call
He's lost, and can't get back at all.

Rupert and the Mystery Pond

He crawls on now, then there's a gleam;
He finds he's gazing in a stream.

And next a giant toad appears,
Who's seen no-one in fifty years.

He says, "This way for Nutwood Lake;
A plunge into that whirlpool take,

And home you'll be in half a twink";
But Rupert feels his courage shrink.

He's told he'll have no time to drown
So trustfully he plunges down,

And wonders where on earth he's gone,
And swirling waters sweep him on.

Then up he's flung with lightning speed,
While round him waggle tongues of weed.

And all at once, to his delight
He's in a pond, in sunshine bright.

Rupert and the Mystery Pond

He looks about him, dripping wet,
And says, "Why, here's the man I met;

"And look, there's father, Bill, the twins!
They're searching for me," Rupert grins.

He shouts, "I'm back, I've had such fun"
And starts to tell what he has done.

But Mr Bear says, "Home you fly,
We'll hear your story when you're dry."

And Mrs Bear says, "Gracious me!
A bath's the thing for you, I see."

Says Rupert, sitting in the steam,
"I've solved the mystery of the stream."

The old explorer, now quite well,
Enjoys the tale he has to tell

And says, "Because you've found the Lake
My stick, as a remembrance take."

metal earth-borers, balloons, kites, clouds and a variety of odd-looking aircraft are frequently at Rupert's disposal. A tiny one-man (or one-bear) helicopter which occasionally appears in the stories was actually designed by a small boy who sent his rough drawing to Bestall. There is also an array of magical footwear to speed passage. The professor's servant possesses a pair of spring-heeled boots which enable the wearer to leap across the forests and lakes of the Nutwood countryside.

But perhaps one of the most charming Bestall inventions was an alternative Underground railway for animals. In one of the very rare instances of a topical event being alluded to in Bestall's era, Rupert somehow found

himself in a crowd watching the Queen's Coronation in 1953. The crowds leaving the processional route poured down into the London Underground, but Rupert was persuaded to descend further than the conventional tube line, and found a lower tunnel where trains were unnecessary, but which yielded rapid access to Nutwood.

Rupert, it should be noted, is an only child – there are no siblings within the bear family. Many of the adventures involve Rupert by himself, but usually one or more of his numerous chums is in attendance. Possibly it is even the chums rather than Rupert himself with whom children most wish to identify. To be part of that incredible circle would be the doorway to an enchanted world full of excitement, wonder and magic.

The torch has been handed on to other artists – Alex Cubie, John Harrold and Lucy Matthews among them. Cubie draws in a vigorous, but much more cartoonlike idiom than Bestall, and his work is usually easily identifiable. Lucy Matthews attempts an imitation of the Bestall style, but what emerges is competent pastiche, no more. John Harrold, on the other hand, has the finer talent, and his work exhibits not only the most imaginative post-Bestall stories, but a high degree of graphic skill, which is his own, not a watered-down copy of his predecessor. In that respect he fits the Bestall attitude when he took over from Mary Tourtel. In collaboration with James Henderson, who has been providing some innovative storylines, such as the replication of the Wise Old Goat into a space colony of countless clones, and a jolly, space-travelling ancient called the Sage of Um, there is proof that Rupert can, after 65 years of continuous existence, carry on for many more.

The *Daily Express* became a tabloid in the late Seventies and changed its ownership. The new shape of the newspaper has wrought certain changes in the presentation of Rupert each day, reflecting the volatile progress of the newspaper, which has made many adjustments, following research. The *Express* and

TEXT CONTINUES ON PAGE 165

Alfred Bestall, when starting up after Mary Tourtel, was asked not to bring magic into the stories, as she overdid it. Ingeniously he got round the restriction by introducing characters such as the Chinese Conjuror, who *had* to use magic.

RUPERT AND THE TRAVEL MACHINE

Says Bill, one day, to Rupert Bear,
"I'd like to take a walk in there."

They see a board which says, "Keep out",
And long to know what it's about.

The naughty chums decide to go,
Although it's wrong, as they well know.

The bushes grow so thick and strong,
They find it hard to get along.

Now as they wonder what to do,
A squirrel asks, "Can I help you?"

He tells them that the road's not far,
So off they run and see a car.

They climb inside, and right away
It starts to move, to their dismay.

The snow is thick upon the ground,
And yet there are no marks around.

The car goes very fast indeed,
And runs towards a shed at speed.

Just as they fear there'll be a smash,
The doors fly open, with a crash.

At once the heavy doors shut tight,
Which gives the startled chums a fright.

Then suddenly, they start to drop,
"Oh dear," sighs Bill, "I'd like to stop."

An angry-looking man draws near,
And says, "I mean to keep you here!"

"You trespassed in my wood," says he,
"So now you both must work for me."

The pals are locked up in a room,
And left to mope there, in the gloom.

The cross old man comes back to ask,
If they are ready for their task.

159

Rupert and the Travel Machine

His new machine they have to test,
And Rupert says, "We'll do our best."

The man now finds a bright, red charm,
And straps it tight on Rupert's arm.

When they are in the huge, steel box,
The old man fastens all the locks.

They're off! and whizzing round and round,
For South Sea Islands they are bound.

The little bear lands in a tree,
Which is as soft as it can be.

When Rupert finds he is alright,
He looks for Bill, who's not in sight.

A monkey speaks to Rupert Bear,
And asks him what he's doing there.

"My chum has gone," sighs Rupert now,
"I've got to find poor Bill, somehow."

Rupert and the Travel Machine

They call and search all round the place,
But of the badger there is no trace.

The monkey climbs the trees so fast
That Rupert takes a fall at last.

"Come back!" he calls, "and help me
please,
I'm not too good at climbing trees."

"I'll ask these birds," says Rupert Bear
"If they have seen Bill any where."

But now the monkey gives a cry,
"Perhaps he's on that land nearby."

The only way to reach the ground,
Is by a vine that they have found.

As soon as they have reached the shore,
The monkey hurries on before.

He soon returns and with him comes,
A turtle who will help the chums.

Rupert and the Travel Machine

Says Mr Turtle, "Come with me;
I'll carry you across the sea."

Just then a bird tells Rupert Bear,
He's seen Bill Badger over there.

The turtle swims so very well,
They feel quite safe upon his shell.

The monkey leaves them both behind,
And runs to see what he can find.

"Look here!" He calls, and Rupert sees
Bill's scarf is hanging in the trees.

Then Rupert finds Bill on the ground,
He seems to be quite safe and sound.

A fearsome savage now springs out,
And scares them with his awful shout.

Soon Bill is caught, and Rupert feels
The ground give way beneath his heels.

The savage grins down at the bear,
For now he knows he's caught the pair.

The chums are tightly tied with rope,
So to escape they cannot hope.

Poor Bill and Rupert walk so far,
They soon lose track of where they are.

The black man spies the coloured charm,
That Rupert wears upon his arm.

Rupert and the Travel Machine

And now, to Rupert's great dismay,
The savage takes the charm away.

When all is quiet, the monkey comes,
To see if he can help the chums.

The monkey chatters with delight,
While he unties the knots so tight.

Then Rupert has a bright idea,
"I know how we can go from here!"

To Bill he quickly tells his plan,
"We'll test that charm now, if we can."

"To Nutwood!" Shouts the little bear,
And straightway they are in the air.

It's snowy still when they get back,
And land by the inventor's shack.

The old man does not see them there,
Until he's called by Rupert Bear.

Rupert and the Travel Machine

"We're back," cries Rupert, "come and see,
The proof that I have brought with me."

"My word!" The old inventor cries,
"This black man is a great surprise."

The savage starts to chase the man,
And so the chums run, while they can.

The old man's workshop is not far,
And there they find the doors ajar.

To the controls they find their way,
And set the dials without delay.

Inside the steel box jump the pair,
To start their journey through the air.

Now, once again, they whirl around,
So very far above the ground.

This time they land at Rupert's door
So thankful to be home once more.

Mail, which went tabloid before it, are as ever locked in the same circulation–advertising struggle that the two newspapers were fighting back in 1920. The present proprietor of the *Express*, Lord Matthews, is as keen a Rupert follower as the first Lord Beaverbrook, and it was on his personal instructions that the bear was incorporated in colour in the *Sunday Express* magazine when it was launched in 1981. Subsequently he has not missed a single issue.

Newspapers are organic creations, and each succeeding issue develops from its predecessor. There is very little that is recognisable in today's *Daily Express* from the big broadsheet newspaper of the Christiansen era, which pioneered striking graphics, bold news displays and a confident editorial touch. There have been changes of editorship in recent years, and an influx of younger editorial executives. Fleet Street has always been a savage commercial battleground, and is now entering a new volatile period in which drastic changes, which have been a long time coming, are now likely to take place in the presentation of daily newspapers. The adoption of new methods of printing and news-gathering, editorial rapid colour, and advanced distribution procedures are inevitable, and nothing is for certain in the changing world. The *Express* management is competitive and dedicated, anxious to reassert the superiority of their newspaper over its rivals, which include the products of newer forces in Fleet Street such as the shrewd and professional Rupert Murdoch and the adventurous Robert Maxwell.

It can, however, be reliably stated that as long as there is a *Daily Express* with Lord Matthews at its helm there will be a Rupert, and that he has merely reached the first 65 years of his existence. Tastes change, it is true, but the odds are on a recognisable Rupert Bear being present in the pages of the first issue of the *Daily Express* to appear in the 21st century.

RUPERT ANNUALS

(A date in brackets denotes original publication in the Daily Express*)*

1936 The New Adventures of Rupert
Rupert and the Wonderful Kite (36)
Rupert, Algy and the Cannibals (36)
Rupert's Autumn Adventure (36)
Rupert, Bill and the Pearls (36)
Rupert's Christmas Adventure
  (35–6)

1937 More Adventures of Rupert
Rupert and the Snow Machine (37)
Rupert and the Flying Bottle (36)
Rupert and the Floods (37)
Rupert and the Little Men (36)
Rupert, Algy and the Smugglers (35)
Rupert and the Chinese Crackers (36)
Rupert and Dog Toby (36)

1938 The New Rupert Book
Rupert and the (Black) Daffodils (37)
 Rupert, Edward and the Paper Chase
  (37)
Rupert in Mysteryland (38)
Rupert and the Ruby Ring (37)
Rupert and the Cuckoo Clock (37–8)
Rupert and Pong Ping (37)
Rupert and Peter (37)
Rupert and Bill in the Treetops (36)

1939 The Adventures of Rupert
Rupert's Adventures in the Snows
  (36)
Rupert and the Jack-in-the-Box
  (38–9)
Rupert's Bonfire (38)
Rupert and the Strange Airman (37)
Rupert and the Half Crowns (37)
Rupert and the Courier Bird (38)
Rupert and the Goblin Cobbler (36–7)
Rupert, Beppo and the Kite (38)

1940 Rupert's Adventure Book
Rupert and Uncle Bruno (38)
Rupert, Bill and the Bluebells (39)
Rupert and the Silver Trowell (38)
Rupert and the Iceberg (38)
Rupert and the Air Smugglers (38)

Rupert's Marvellous Bat (39)
Rupert and King Frost (39)
Rupert and the Pedlar (38)

1941 The Rupert Book
Rupert and the Red Egg (40)
Rupert and the Baby Badger (38)
Rupert and the Mystery Pond (39)
Rupert and the Forest Fire (40)
Rupert and the Lost Boat (39)
Rupert and the Little Woodman (39)
Rupert and the Sugar Bird (39)

1942 More Adventures of Rupert
(Paperback)
Rupert and the Cartwheels (40)
Rupert and the Odmedod (40)
Rupert and the Wrong Presents
  (39–40)
Rupert and the Old Ruin (39)
Rupert and the Little Plane (41)
Rupert and the Sea Serpent (39)
Rupert and the Fire (37)
Rupert at Sandy Bay (38)

1943 More Rupert Adventures
Rupert and the Circus Dog (41)
Rupert and the Piper (40)
Rupert and the Banjo (40)
Rupert's Good Turn (40)
Rupert and Tiger Lily (40)
Rupert's Birthday (41)
Rupert and the Iron Key (41)
Rupert and Golly (41–2)
Rupert and the Black Moth (41)
Rupert's Big Game Hunt (41)
Rupert's River Adventure (41)

1944 Rupert in More Adventures
Rupert and Rollo (42)
Rupert and the Old Map (42)
Rupert and the Tiny Flute (42)
Rupert and the Mystery Voice (42)
Rupert and the Yellow Cloak
Rupert and Snuffy
Rupert and Granny Goat (43)

Rupert's Rainy Adventure (42)
Rupert's Strange Party (42)
Rupert and the Dutch Doll (40–1)

1945 A New Rupert Book
Rupert and the Reindeer (42–3)
Rupert and the Cuckoo (43)
Rupert and the Turnips (43)
Rupert and Jock (43)
Rupert and Willie (43)
Rupert's Fairy Cycle (43–4)
Rupert and the Music Man (44)
Rupert's Winter Journey (43)
Rupert and Bingo's Trail

1946 New Rupert Book
Rupert on Coon Island
Rupert and Rastus (44)
Rupert and the Blue Mountain (44)
Rupert and the Prince of China
Rupert, Beppo and the Duck (44)
Rupert and Podgy (44)
Rupert and the Rocket Plane
Rupert and Bingo (45)
Rupert and the Magic Dart (44–5)

1947 More Adventures of Rupert
Rupert and the Top Hat (45)
Rupert and the Black Cat (45)
Rupert and the Young Dragon (45)
Rupert, Bill and the Merboy (45)
Rupert and the Paper Kettle
Rupert and the Woffle Fly
Rupert and Koko (45)
Rupert and the Wavy Wand
Rupert's Christmas Tree (45–6)

1948 The Rupert Book
Rupert and Jack Frost (46)
Rupert and the Blue Balloon
Rupert and the Magic Stock
Rupert and the Sleepy Pears (46)
Rupert and Rosalie
Rupert and the Rainbow
Rupert's Puppy Hunt (46)
Rupert and Cedric

Rupert and the Hobby-Horse

Alfred Bestall with one of his young readers, the author's son and adviser Matthew Perry.

1960 Rupert
Rupert and the Crystal
Rupert and Morwenna (52)
Rupert and Ozzie (53)
Rupert and the Diamond Leaf (52)

1961 Rupert
Rupert and the Hearth-Rug
Rupert and the Pepper Rose (53)
Rupert and the Black Spark (53)
Rupert and the New Boat (54–5)
Rupert and Greyrocks Cove (54)

1962 Rupert
Rupert and the Dragon Fly
Rupert and the Robins (52–3)
Rupert and Niagara (54)
Rupert and the Bad Dog (53)
Rupert and the Coral Island (53)

1963 Rupert
Rupert and the Birthday Present
Rupert and the Golden Acorn (55)
Rupert and the Lost Cuckoo (53)
Rupert and the Inventor (54)
Rupert and the Cold-Cure (55)

1964 Rupert
Rupert and the Dover Sole
Rupert and the Distant Music (55)
Rupert and the Compass (53)
Rupert and the Dog-Roses (56)
Rupert and the Rock Pool (56)

1965 Rupert
Rupert and the Gaffer
Rupert and the Winter Woolley (56)
Rupert and the Old Hat (57)
Rupert and Rusty (57)

1966 Rupert
Rupert and the Magic Ball (54)
Rupert and the Secret Boat (58)
Rupert and the Billy Goat (54)
Rupert and the Spring Chicken (54)

1967 Rupert
Rupert and the Lost List (57–8)
Rupert and the Jackdaw (58)
Rupert and Floppity (58)
Rupert and the Carved Stick (58)

1968 Rupert
Rupert and the Truant (58–9)
Rupert and the Fiddle (57)
Rupert and the Fire-Bird (56)
Rupert and the Rolling Ball (57)

1969 Rupert
Rupert and the Whistlefish (59)
Rupert and the Old Chimney (55–6)
Rupert and the Snowball (59)
Rupert and Raggety (59)
Rupert and the Fishing Rod (56)

1970 Rupert
Rupert and the Outlaws (59)
Rupert and the Blunderpuss (58)
Rupert and the Paper-Fall (60–1)
Rupert and the Sky-Boat (60)

1971 Rupert
Rupert and the Gomnies (60)
Rupert and the Popweed (61)
Rupert and the Early Bird (58)
Rupert and the Windlings (59–60)

1972 Rupert
Rupert's Deep Sea Adventure (55)
Rupert and the Learner (62)
Rupert and the Rugger Match (61)
Rupert and Gwyneth (60)

1973 Rupert
Rupert and the Bouncers (61–2)
Rupert and the Housemouse (61)
Rupert and the Waterfall (62)
Rupert and the Flying Boat (61)

1974 Rupert
Rupert and the Iron Spade (63)
Rupert and Jenny Frost (63)
Rupert and the Secret Path (61)
Rupert and the Little Bells (62–3)

1975 Rupert
Rupert and the Little River (63)
Rupert and the Thinking Cap (56–7)
Rupert and the Broken Plate (54)
Rupert and the Blue Star (60)
Rupert and the Winter Sale (60)

1976 Rupert
Rupert and the Jumping Men (64)
Rupert and Young Kevin (65)
Rupert and the Hot Water (62)
Rupert and the Windy Day (56)

1977 Rupert
Rupert and the Winkybickies (65)
Rupert and the Fire-Lighter (63)
Rupert and Septimus (63)
Rupert and the Silent Land (57)

1978 Rupert
Rupert and the Rivals (63)
Rupert and the Squire (59)
Rupert and the Boffit (65)
Rupert and the Secret Shell (65)
Rupert's Odd Party (64–5)

1979 Rupert
Rupert and the Penguins (66)
Rupert and the Moon Moths (66)
Rupert and the Ice Skates (65–6)
Rupert and the Capricorn (66)

1980 Rupert
Rupert and the Flavours (72)
Rupert and the Mixed Magic (72–3)
Rupert and the Blizzard (66–7)
Rupert and the Ocean Office (68)

1981 Rupert
Rupert and the Castle Trap (72)
Rupert and the Wicked Uncle (51)
Rupert and the Buzzing Box (51)
Rupert and the Wrong Sweets (64)
Rupert and the Silent Dog (52)
Rupert and the Baby Cloud (60)

1982 Rupert
Rupert and Pong-Ping (37)
Rupert and the Umbrella Boy (65)
Rupert and the Gemlins (66)
Rupert and the Snow Puzzle (71)
Rupert and the Red Box (38)

1983 Rupert
Rupert and the Black Circle
Rupert and the Dragon Race
Rupert and Santa Paws
Rupert's Autumn Adventure

1984 Rupert
Rupert and the Two Moons
Rupert and the Wee Man
Rupert and the Igloo
Rupert and the Wonderful Kite
Rupert and the Cuckoo Clock

1985 Rupert
Rupert, Bill and the Pearls
Rupert at Pong-Ping's Party
Rupert and the Unknown Journey
Rupert and the Snowstorm
Rupert and the Pirate Boys
Rupert and the Windmill